HUMBUGS AND DOODLEBUGS

A Wartime Story of Seaside Sweetmakers

STEPHEN JAMES KING

Copyright © Stephen James King, 2019
Published by I_AM Self-Publishing, 2019.

The right of Stephen James King to be identified as the Author of the Work has been asserted by him in accordance with the Copyright, Designs and Patents Act 1988.

All rights reserved.

ISBN 978-1-913036-25-6

This book is sold subject to the condition it shall not, by way of trade or otherwise, be circulated in any form or by any means, electronic or otherwise without the publisher's prior consent.

@iamselfpub
www.iamselfpublishing.com

Dedication

To Lucas, Zachary, Freya, Anwyn and Lowen. Always a joy to their Grandpa.

Sweetmaker, Sergeant Stanley King in December 1945, aged thirty-four and looking pleased as his four and a half years in the army will soon be over.

A carefree-looking Doris, aged twenty-five in 1938, two years before her marriage to Stan. She could not have foreseen that the joy of married life would be coupled with the uncertainty and loneliness of wartime. This photograph hung on our lounge wall throughout my childhood.

Contents

Introduction: Surprise discovery, unanswered questions. 7
1. Stan and Doris, who were they?..................................13
2. The 1930s. Meeting Doris and making sweets. 20
3. 1939–40. Being bombed and getting married. 34
4. 1941. White aprons and humbugs, to khaki and engines. 46
5. 1942–43. The joy of parenthood and the tragedy of war. 52
6. 1944. Landing in Normandy, delivering in Rochford. 66
7. 1945. War ends, separation doesn't. 98
8. 1946. Back to normal life: death, illness, work and family. 110
9. 1947 onwards. The family is complete but are dreams fulfilled? 114
10. 2013. Following Father's footsteps. 124

Introduction: Surprise discovery, unanswered questions.

Why this story should be told.

The six years from 1939 were like no other period in British history.

There has not been a conflict, before or since, that has touched every aspect of daily life in Britain, as did World War II.

This is the story of my parents, Stan and Doris King, during that very difficult time. It is set in a seaside town where they started a sweet-making business. It describes the challenges they faced, from raising children while under the daily risk of bombing to being a soldier in the Allied invasion of Europe. What Stan and Doris went through was not exceptional for the period, but it is a personal story and therefore unique and needs to be told lest it be forgotten by future generations. What little they told me of the war I have included, and the remainder is the result of my research.

I hope you will enjoy reading their story.

Surprise discovery.

It was December 1940; the Second World War had been raging for over a year.

The German Army had occupied most of Europe, and Adolf Hitler, the German dictator, was determined that Britain would be next. That summer had seen the 'Battle of Britain' take place in the skies over southern England. The German air force (the Luftwaffe) had been trying to obliterate the Royal Air Force so that the German Army could invade Britain. Stan and Doris had probably watched 'dog fight' battles between Messerschmitts and Spitfires over Southend in the summer skies.

After a hot, dry summer, winter was cold with little sunshine. In the late afternoon of Wednesday 11th December, twenty-nine-year-old Stan walked the mile and a half home from his sweet factory in Shoe Lane. As he walked along the London Road, he would have been aware of many empty houses and shops and some bomb-damaged buildings. The risk of a German invasion had resulted in thousands of residents leaving the town for safer parts of the country.

After arriving home at 44 Mount Avenue, Westcliff-on-Sea, he changed out of his cornflour dusted clothes. One feature of the boiled-sweet-making process was that the sweets were sticky as they cooled. To avoid the sweets sticking to working surfaces they had to be dusted with cornflour. This resulted in his clothes and glasses being covered in a white dust. Once out of his work clothes, Stan sat in the lounge with Doris to hear the six o'clock news on the BBC. The news was no better than the previous night.

The German air force was continuing its 'Blitz' (intense and frequent bombing intended to bring about a swift German victory) of British cities, with its main focus on London. Stan and Doris could see and hear the German bombers and fighter escorts flying along the Thames to attack the docks and the industrial and residential areas of the capital city.

The windows of their house were draped with blackout curtains so that no light could be seen outside that might attract the enemy pilots. Stan and Doris had only married six months earlier and the house at Mount Avenue was their first home together. It was a smart, modern, detached house that they had probably been able to rent at a reasonable price due to the high number of empty properties in the town. It was halfway down a hill leading to Chalkwell Station with a view of the River Thames. This should have been an idyllic, romantic time for Stan and his new bride, but not on that Wednesday evening.

At 9.15 pm the Southend air raid sirens blared out their warning sound. Anti-aircraft fire could be heard as German bombers flew over the town. This was nothing unusual that autumn and winter, and the newlyweds probably did not bother to go to an air raid shelter (they never mentioned using one). The next thing they heard was an enormous explosion and felt an air pressure shockwave that made their ears go pop. The house shook, and the windows rattled. A fifty-kilogram high explosive bomb exploded in Mount Avenue only yards from their home.

They waited a few moments in case there were further explosions and then ran outside to see if anyone was hurt. Fortunately, no one was injured and there was no serious damage to their house. Air raid wardens and the police soon arrived. They checked for casualties and assessed the damage so that they could make an official report to the authorities.

The following day, Stan went to work as usual at the sweet factory, while Doris was back behind the counter at the sweet shop they had opened on the London Road near the factory. Life had to go on regardless of the war.

The really surprising aspect of this bomb explosion to me is that Stan and Doris, my father and mother, never mentioned this apparent close shave with death to their children. Much of the above description is therefore based on how I imagine what would have happened, from my knowledge of my parents in later life. It may be my parents did not talk about this incident because they were traumatised by it or unable to put their experience into words. However, with my understanding of their characters, I doubt this. More likely, I suspect, they did not talk much about the war because they were so involved with raising three children, running an expanding business and too busy on day to day life issues to dwell on the past.

How do I know about the bomb in Mount Avenue?

It was over seventy years later that I discovered this dramatic event. I was at the Essex Records Office in Chelmsford following up my interest in the Second World War. The archivist had brought me a large road map dating from the war, which was now creased and faded. It was the official map on which was marked the location of every one of the 800 bombs that exploded on the Borough of Southend-on-Sea during the war. I looked at the map to check whether any bombs landed near where my parents lived or worked. I was shocked to discover that bomb number 333 was shown as exploding near to 44 Mount Avenue, where I knew Mum and Dad were living at the time. I was amazed because they never said anything about a bomb explosion near their house, so I wondered why they never talked about this 'life and death' incident.

Curiosity awakened, so many unanswered questions.

I felt regretful that I knew so little about their war experiences, but my curiosity was awakened. Suddenly there was a whole period of my parents' lives that I knew little about. It was too late to ask them, they had both passed away over thirty years before. I felt sad that I had not asked them more. My eldest brother, John, had also passed away, and there was no close relative still alive who had lived through that period. My elder brother, Michael, was fortunately able to join me on discovering some of how they lived.

I only had a sketchy knowledge of their life in WWII. I knew that Mum lived in an invasion risk area subject to heavy bombing. Dad spent almost five years of his life as a soldier, including taking part in the liberation of Europe. Yet, to me, they were happy, well-adjusted people without any apparent psychological scars from the war or even much interest in it. They certainly showed no hatred of the German people, as other people of their generation I have known have shown.

But I wanted to understand what life was like for them living through such a dangerous, uncertain and dramatic six years, the like of which my and later generations have not experienced. I was determined to find out more.

But how did this conflict affect their lives and family?

What did Stan do and where did he go in the five years he was in the army?

How did Doris cope with the bombing, helping to run a business, food rationing and motherhood?

Why, to their children, did they seem unaffected by the war?

And why did they not talk about it very much?

I wanted to find out the answers to these and many more questions. And, in writing this account of their wartime lives, I wanted to pay my respects and show my appreciation to my parents for what they did and who they were.

My quest for more knowledge had begun.

Playground games for my generation, fear and tragedy for my parents' generation.

Whilst World War II apparently held little fascination for Stan and Doris, it certainly did and still does for many 'Baby Boomers', that generation born just after the war. I remember in my junior school playground playing war games of 'German and British soldiers', which was a rather one-sided game as we all wanted to be the British. Also, a common question amongst my school friends was 'what did your dad do in the war?', with each of us trying to surpass the other with more impressive stories of the wartime deeds of our fathers. The baby boomers' fascination with the war has continued as they seek to understand events that took place just before they were born. Events that were much more momentous than those that have taken place in their own lifetimes.

INTRODUCTION: SURPRISE DISCOVERY, UNANSWERED QUESTIONS.

It has been said that the Second World War, 1939 to 1945, was the only 'just' war in history. What this means is that the conflict was undertaken by Britain and the United States in order to free the peoples of Europe from a military dictator and to end ethnic genocide. By 1945 the Nazis, due to their ideological beliefs, had deliberately murdered over six million people, mainly Jewish, just because of their race and religion. If they had not been stopped, they would have killed millions more. As it was, this world conflict resulted in the deaths of over sixty million people.

The period of the Second World War was the last, and arguably the only occasion, where the whole country was at total war. Everyone was affected. At home, amongst other deprivations, people were being bombed, deprived of food and having to mourn loved ones. Men were required to put on hold their careers and go into the military to fight for the very survival of their country, knowing that if they failed an English way of life built up over hundreds of years and the freedoms that went with it would be lost. Women delayed marriage and having children; instead they did war work in factories, on farms or took over many of the other jobs usually done by men in peacetime. The generations born since 1945 have not known the same uncertainty each day as to whether you or a loved one would be killed, either by bombing at home or in military action abroad.

My father, Stanley King, was an ordinary soldier, one of 3,788,000 others that served in the British Army. They all made sacrifices of one sort or another to defend Britain and democracy. Stan spent almost five years in the prime of his life assisting the war effort. He was separated from his new wife for long periods and lost his only brother, who was killed in 1942. Doris gave birth to two children without her husband being around to support her, and Stan did not see his son, Michael, until he was almost a year old.

1. Stan and Doris, who were they?

Stan and Doris are: the parents of John, Michael and Stephen; the grandparents of Paul, Daniel, Natasha, Heidi, Trevor, Leane and Darren; and the great grandparents of Lucas, Zachary, Freya, Chloe, Evelyn, Charlotte, Nathan, Ryan, Alfie, Freddie, Grace, Morgan, Anwyn and Lowen.

Stan and Doris's parents and grandparents

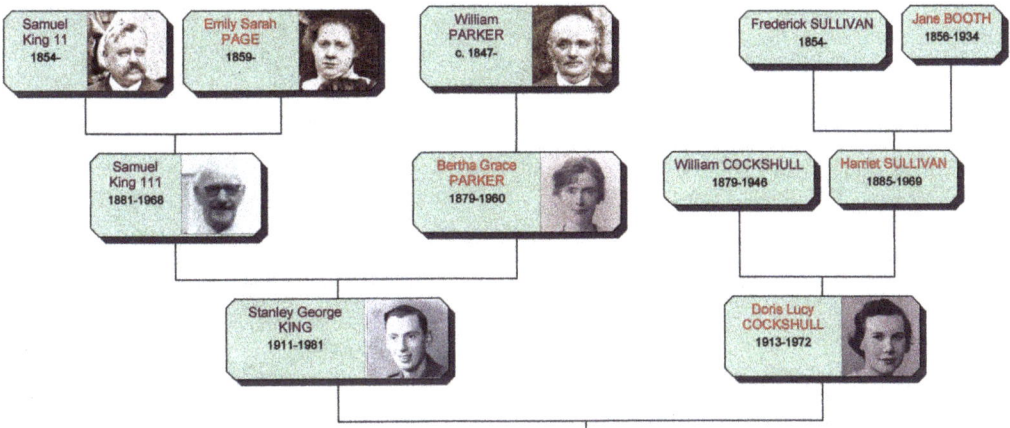

The photograph was probably taken in 1915 so that Samuel, my grandfather, could take a picture of his family with him to France in World War One. It shows Grace, aged thirty-six; Jim, eight; Stanley, four; and Samuel, thirty-four. Samuel is wearing the uniform of the Royal Army Service Corps, the same Corps that Stan would join some twenty-six years later. On a visit to Toronto in the 1990s to see Stan's cousin Mabel, she told me that there was a family story about this photograph. Apparently, there was an argument about Stan wearing the boots that had previously belonged to his brother Jim.

Stanley ('Stan') George King was born on 23rd September 1911 (probably in Harrow Weald, Middlesex) to Samuel and Bertha Grace King (nee Parker). Stan had an elder brother, James, born in 1909. Samuel was a chauffeur, although he had also most likely been employed in his father's (also a Samuel) confectionery business, which was set up in 1878. Samuel Senior was born in Lambeth in 1854. Bertha Grace comes from a long line (so far traced back to the 1690s) of Parkers who were farmers or agricultural labourers in the Swaffham Prior area of Cambridgeshire. I remember Stan in his middle-aged years as being very tall with thick brown hair, athletic muscular build, large hands, and feet needing size twelve shoes. He was slimmer in his younger years – his army pay-book describes him, at aged thirty, as being nine stone eleven pounds with a 35-inch chest and 5 feet 11.5 inches tall with brown eyes.

He had a good sense of humour and a keen interest in people, always finding time to chat to the man in the local garage or off licence. His school reports show he was clever at school and he retained an enquiring mind later in life. For example, I remember in his sixties him becoming interested in the unusual patterns on the land that had been revealed by aerial photographs of South America. Daily newspapers kept him up to date with the world, and he usually had an opinion on current issues. He was very resourceful and practical, and no job was too difficult for him to tackle, be it building large sheds or putting in central heating.

Stan as a boy on a homemade car with brother, Jim, behind and parents, Samuel and Bertha Grace. The handles Stan is holding may be a steering device operated by string attached to the front crossbar, or they could be brakes rubbing against the back wheels. Probably taken around 1918, which would make Stan seven and Jim nine.

Doris Lucy King (nee Cockshull) was born on 31st July 1913 in Peckham (South London) to William and Harriet Cockshull (nee Sullivan). Doris had one sister, Harriet, nine years her senior, whose father always called her Queenie, and this is the name she used all her life. Harriet Senior had the dual role of bringing up her two daughters and running the family ironmongers' shop in Lordship Lane, Dulwich. William was a carpenter, although it is believed he was hospitalised in a mental institution for long periods. Of Doris's grandfathers, one was a plumber the other a calico glazer (a process of putting a high lustre or glaze on cotton material – *rootschat.com*). Doris was medium height, smartly dressed and quick thinking. She was very supportive of her husband and children and an equal intellectual partner with Stan in the sweet business. She was very practical and hardworking and never complained about the relentless domestic tasks involved in looking after a large family. She was assertive when she needed to be, as when she phoned my school headmaster to turn up the heating when I complained that the classroom was cold. She was an excellent ballroom dancer, keen on dressmaking and knitting, and a passionate gardener. I could tell Stan and Doris loved each other by the way they looked at each other, the way Dad spoke warmly and in a complimentary way about Mum, and the way they very rarely disagreed with each other.

My mother, Doris Lucy Cockshull, as a child. I'm not sure how old she is here. What do you think? The picture was taken in a photographer's studio, where they would have provided the tennis racquet she is holding and the ball at her feet.

Doris at the seaside, probably in her early twenties, which would date this to the early 1930s. She is wearing an eye-catching jacket and trouser outfit. She is with her sister, Queenie, who is nine years older than her.

Doris as a pretty young woman in a dress she made herself (according to her sister, Queenie).

2. The 1930s. Meeting Doris and making sweets.

Stan's education and apprenticeship disappointments.

Stan's school reports show that he was an able pupil, consistently coming top of the class at Harrow Weald Council School. When he left Waller Road secondary school in New Cross aged fourteen, his headmaster said he 'showed great ability and intelligence'. His educational prowess resulted in him being offered a subsidised place at the prestigious Dulwich College. Stan told me that his parents could not afford the fees, even though they were discounted by half, so he left school without any qualifications.

Now that higher education was closed off to him, he had to consider other paths for his future. His father was a chauffeur, and his grandfather had owned motor cars and vans, so Stan already knew a lot about cars. The first mass production motor car, the Model T Ford, had revolutionised motoring in the 1920s and car ownership was rapidly expanding. Stan decided that motor mechanics would be a good career option. This resulted in an apprenticeship at a local garage. But world events were to intervene.

The Wall Street Financial Crash of 1929 had precipitated the Great Depression of the early 1930s, when some three million people in the UK were unemployed. When he completed his apprenticeship, he was sacked by his employer, as the garage owner could not afford to pay the wages of a fully qualified mechanic. Work was very difficult to find and there were few vacancies for mechanics. It is not known for how long Stan was unemployed.

It is unclear what work Stan did after the end of his garage apprenticeship in the early 1930s, but it is believed that his father was now running a sweet factory in South London, so Stan may well have gone to work for him

(I recall hearing references around the dining room table when I was young to a sweet factory being next to Sam King Junior's house in Pendrell Road in South London). The confectionery business experience of his father and grandfather was to prove very useful to him. By the late 1930s he was seriously considering starting his own sweet-making business.

\multicolumn{4}{l}{**MIDDLESEX EDUCATION COMMITTEE.**}

MIDDLESEX EDUCATION COMMITTEE.
Harrow Weald Council School. Boys' Department.
REPORT for Term ended Easter 1924
Name Stanley King   Class I Std VI

SUBJECT	Marks p'ssible	Marks gained	REMARKS	SUBJECT	Marks p'ssible	Marks gained	REMARKS
Scripture	10	9		Physical Exercises	10	6	
Reading	10	8		Drawing Pen.	10	9	
Arithmetic Prob.	10	8		Paint	10	8	
Composition	10	8		Mental Arith.	10	8	
Writing and Dictation	10	10		Arith Mech. Domestic Science	10	2	
Grammar	10	8		Needlework Position		1st	
Geography	15	12		Cookery No. in Class		8	
History	10	8		General Progress		Excellent	
Recitation	10	6		Conduct		Excellent	
Nature & Object Lessons	10	9		Attendance			

REMARKS:—   Times absent 16   late /
Class Teacher _____   Head Teacher _____
Report Received Grace King   Parent or Guardian.

Twelve-year-old Stan's school report. He was consistently top of the class during his school days, although perhaps competition was not that great at a small country school. Did having three weeks absence, probably due to sickness, result in him struggling with mechanical arithmetic? My daughter Heidi and I visited Stan's cousins, Mabel and Grace, in Toronto in the late 1990s. Grace mentioned that Stan had a stammer when he was young, which came as a complete surprise to me as I had never heard him struggle with his speech. Was Stan's poor mark for recitation on his school report a result of his youthful stammer?

Tall and handsome, own car, lots of friends.

Stan talked little to my brothers and I about his social life in the period before he got married. This is understandable as my mother was unlikely to have wanted to hear about his good times with earlier girlfriends. However, after he died, I discovered amongst his belongings several photographs showing him with groups of smiling male and female friends. These photographs were taken at some of the early holiday camps on the east coast of Norfolk or Suffolk. Views of him standing happily next to attractive young ladies show that he was having the time of his life.

A young man with his own motor car was quite a social asset before the war. He kept in contact with his cousins in the Babraham and Pampisford area of Cambridgeshire and they were not averse to a little 'high jinks'. For example, years later, when I visited his cousin Mabel in Toronto, she recalled with laughter in her voice an amusing incident. Apparently, after the marriage of one of their cousins, the bride and groom retired back to their farm. So, late in the evening, a few of the cousins, including Stan and Mabel, crept up to their house and threw pebbles up at the bridal bedroom window to disturb their wedding night.

Quickstep to falling in love.

Stan and Doris were both good ballroom dancers. I remember as a boy, when going on our annual holiday to a Butlins holiday camp, Mum and Dad would take part in the ballroom dancing competition. Dad would be wearing a smart suit and shiny black shoes and Mum a pretty dress. They would glide around the floor, doing a waltz or foxtrot in perfect harmony, with not a missed step the whole way around. They would usually get to the final few in the competition, despite this being their only dance outing of the year. We boys were not left out on these evenings as Mum would take us on to the dance floor to try and teach us the steps and rhythm of the waltz.

To get to a good standard, Stan would needed to have spent many evenings at various dance halls, having lessons, perfecting his steps and enjoying the company of many young ladies. Did dancing bring Stan and Doris together? Doris had been a keen dancer from a young age, as shown in a school dancing class photo that I have. She may have been influenced by her older sister, Queenie, also a good dancer, who in the 1950s had wanted to open a dancing school at her home in Finchley Road, Westcliff-on-Sea. Certainly, Doris would have attracted Stan with her dancing skills. I have Doris's bronze and silver dancing medals from the Imperial Society of Teachers of Dancing, which testify to her expertise.

Doris and Stan having fun at the seaside in their courting days, probably in the summer of 1938. Doris wears fashionable beach clothing while Stan has a smart car, which is likely to be a 1934 2 litre Morris 6 with a freewheel gearbox, picnic tables in the rear but only one windscreen wiper. Stan had probably borrowed his father's car to impress his girlfriend rather than use his own rather cramped Austin 7 Convertible.

As they only lived some two miles apart, Stan in Camberwell off the Old Kent Road and Doris in Lordship Lane, Dulwich, it was probably only a matter of time before they would meet at a local dancing venue. Doris was pretty, stylish and well dressed. Stan was six feet tall and handsome and he owned an Austin 7 Convertible, even if it was rather small and had no heater. They must have been an impressive-looking couple. As well as enjoying dancing together, they enjoyed all the benefits of living in London, including watching the latest Fred Astaire and Ginger Rogers films and regular trips to the theatre. Indeed, Doris's prize possession was a pair of silver opera glasses (I still have these), which she used to get a better view of the performance.

I remember them saying that one of their favourite entertainment places was the Trocadero in Leicester Square. I had the impression from them that this was a dance hall. However, research on the *arthurlloyd.co.uk* website shows it to have been mainly a Lyons Restaurant with cabaret shows. These were carefree, happy days for the couple. How they must have enjoyed trips down to Southend to plan their future life together. Stan proposed and gave Doris a lovely single diamond gold engagement ring that she wore for the rest of her life.

Stan and Doris walking up Pier Hill, Southend-on-Sea, in their carefree single days before the war. Perhaps they were planning their future life in Southend. Judging from the smile on Doris's face, this was a happy time for the young lovers.

Drive to reach the top but falling off on the way.

Stan had a dream of becoming a successful businessman. This was made clear to my brothers and I by a story he told about his new motorcycle. He bought a brand-new Ivory Calthorpe (the sloping engine model was made between 1930 and 1937) and decided to take it on a long journey. He rode it all the way to the Scottish Highlands, which must have been quite an adventure in the days before motorways or town bypasses when poor roads made punctures a common occurrence. What had impressed him, however, on his Scottish journey was a wonderful hotel in the beautiful Trossachs area of the Highlands. It was far too expensive for him to stay in; however, he vowed to himself that, one day in the future, when he had made his fortune, he would drive back to Scotland in a Rolls Royce and stay in the best room in that five-star hotel. A dream that probably fuelled his ambition.

His return journey was uneventful until he was nearly home. As he crossed London Bridge, he twice skidded on the wet, autumn leaves and fell off. It amused him that he had managed to stay upright on his motorbike for hundreds of miles on unfamiliar roads only to lose control, and slide along the tarmac on his bottom, on a road near home that he knew so well. It is interesting that he had a humorous reaction to what was probably a frightening experience. Perhaps this attitude helped him to cope with some of the disturbing sights he must have witnessed during the war.

Stan's grandfather spots a business opportunity.

Was Stan's choice of career influenced by his grandfather's success in business? Stan would have known his grandfather quite well as he lived until Stan was seventeen years old. Stories would have been told around the dining table of Samuel Snr's successful sweet-making business and Stan would have seen the photographs of him driving smart motor cars. Samuel Senior was born in Lambeth in January 1854, the son of another Samuel who was a cutter/turner (he probably made items on a lathe). It is not known how he was able to start up his own business or what experience or training he had had. He married eighteen-year-old Emily Page in March 1877 at St James's Church, Piccadilly, and Sam Junior (Stan's father) was born in 1881, the third of ten children.

In the 18th century, sweet-making was generally confined to the upper classes where large houses would have separate rooms, often referred to as 'The Confectionery', where sweet treats were prepared. By the early 19th century, some high street bakery/confectionery shops were producing sweets for the middle classes. Several factors were to make sweets readily available to all classes of the population.

After 1850, synthetic flavours became available. Prince Albert's Great Exhibition of 1851 showcased a whole variety of boiled sweets to the general public. By the late 19th century, new machinery was becoming available to mass produce sweets. Probably the most significant change was in 1874 when the tax on sugar imports was lifted, significantly reducing prices. Four years later, twenty-four-year-old Samuel King Senior started his sweet-making business somewhere, it is believed, in the Holborn area of London. It was in 1878 (according to Stan) that Samuel Senior opened a bank account with the forerunner of Midland Bank (a bank that the next three generations also used).

By 1881 the family had moved to Norwich Court in the City of London. We do not know what kind of confectionery Samuel started making but it is probable that it was boiled sweets, as this is what Stan went on to make. Sam Senior was clearly a successful businessman as, by 1901, he was the proud owner of one of the earliest motor cars, a French Darracq. He died in 1929, aged seventy-five, and left £982 in his will, enough to buy two average houses.

Trappings of business success. Samuel King Senior, Stan's grandfather, at the wheel of his 1902 Darracq with his wife, Emily. The only weather protection was a rug that can be seen dangling at the back of the car.

It does not seem that Samuel Junior (Stan's father) initially worked in the sweet business as, up to about 1923, he was working as a chauffeur and living at Hermitage Cottage, Harold Weald in what was then rural Middlesex. However, by 1925 he and his family had moved to Pendrell Road, Brockley SE4, and at this point he may well have taken over the confectionery business from his father. Stan said he loved living in the country in Middlesex and did not like it at all having to move into the crowded urban environment of South London. (Another of Stan's ambitions was to live in the countryside once again, which he did later in life.) A couple of years later, the family moved again, to Sylvan Grove SE15, where it is believed they had a sweet factory next to their house.

Is this the same vehicle as in the previous photograph, except that it has been converted into a van? The wheels and bonnet look the same as Sam King Senior's 1902 Darracq.
This is Sam King Senior with his confectionery business delivery van. The man on the right of the picture is probably Sam King Junior and the boy may be his son, Jim (Stan's brother). If this supposition is correct the picture would be from about 1912, when Sam Senior would have been fifty-eight, Sam Junior thirty-one and Jim five years old.

'Cokernut' toffee at the seaside.

Stan had trained as a motor mechanic, but he could not get a job that paid a qualified mechanic's wages. The Great Depression, otherwise called the great slump, of the 1930s was the worst economic calamity of the 20th century. Unemployment caused severe hardship, particularly as welfare benefits were meagre. Some 22% of workers did not have a job in 1932 and, by 1936, 13% were still out of work. Memories of this period influenced Stan for the rest of his life. He would tell his children: 'be prepared; there will be another slump' meaning that good times do not last. Also, he referred to the family house in Barling, near Southend, that he purchased for cash in the 1950s, as his 'bolthole' should his business ventures go sour.

It is not known what job Stan had in the early 1930s, during the worst of the Great Depression, following being made redundant after his motor mechanic training. His father was probably running the sweet-making business in South London at this time and Stan may have been working with him. This would explain where he gained his knowledge of the confectionery trade. In 1937, Stan was twenty-five years old and around this time he decided to start his own confectionery business with his brother, Jim, as his partner. He was determined to make his new venture a success, after the earlier disappointments of not being able to go to a good school and of being made redundant from his chosen profession in the motor trade. His cousins in Cambridgeshire were now becoming successful farmers and, I suspect, Stan wanted to keep up with them. He did everything he could to make this new venture flourish.

Stan and Jim first had to decide the best location for a sweet factory. London was the obvious choice as his grandfather had been running a successful business there. But perhaps the future lay in producing sweets for the seaside trade, to cope with the growing numbers of leisure visitors to coastal resorts. Southend-on-Sea was one of the closest seaside resorts to London and was linked to the capital by two mainline railways and the country's first dual carriageway road, the A127 Southend Arterial Road. The town was expanding quickly and was just the place a new business could grow. By starting his business in Southend, Stan could break away from what his father and grandfather had done and run his business the way he wanted to. By the late 1930s, Stan had met his future wife, Doris, and the thought of starting family life in attractive seaside surroundings was probably on his mind. According to his driving licence, he was still living in Sylvan Grove,

Peckham in 1937, although his business accounts show he was working in Southend during that year.

Stan and Jim found some premises on the first floor of a small building in Shoe Lane at the rear of 488 London Road, Westcliff-on-Sea. (The building was still there in 2015, although in a dilapidated condition.) They carried sugar boiling equipment, sweet moulds, ingredients, display boxes and labels up the outside staircase and set to work. As well as making the sweets, they had to visit local shops and wholesalers to try to sell their products.

The first set of accounts is for the period up to 31st January 1938. The trading, profit and loss accounts and balance sheet are beautifully written up in Doris's own handwriting. Doris was providing considerable accounting help to the fledgling business some two years before she married. Stan had not only found the love of his life but also a very capable business partner.

Stan and Jim put up capital of £445 to start the business, which was quite a sum in those days, certainly enough to buy a house in those depressed times. How did they raise this amount of money? Perhaps it was a gift from his parents, or they could have been left money in his grandfather's will, or prudently saved money themselves from previous jobs. The accounts for their first year of trading show sales of £465, with a net loss for the period of £25. They took a wage of £3 per week shared between them.

The following year sales had doubled to £933 and Stan and Jim were now employing staff as salaries were £171, although the business still made a loss of £10. Their mother, Bertha Grace King, leant the business £35, presumably to allow them to have enough cash for day-to-day operations. The year to January 1940 was the first year of profit, with a sum of thirty-one pounds, sixteen shillings and eight and a half pence.

In the year before Stan's call up to the army, profits rose ten times to £383. This was over twice the level of average national earnings and could have provided a 70% deposit on the cost of the average house (£545 in 1938). So, with a prosperous and rapidly expanding business, there is no doubt that the war came at an inconvenient time.

How did Stan and Jim sell the sweets they were making? Fortunately, the account day-book still survives that records all the transaction of their early business. Sweets were sold to several Southend wholesalers who then distributed them to the many sweet shops in and around the town. Confectionery wholesalers were still active well into the 1960s, when Stan's son, John, my brother, worked for a time for such a firm (called Marsh's) based at the corner of Southchurch Road and Hamstel Road. Another outlet was a shop they rented on the London Road, between Brightwell Avenue and Ramuz Drive, to sell sweets directly to the public.

Doris's unknown skill. These are Stan and Jim's final accounts for their first year of trading up to 31st January 1938. By comparing the handwriting in her diaries, I deduced that the accounts were prepared by Doris. She never spoke of her expertise in double-entry bookkeeping and final accounts, even when, later on, she was helping Michael and me with our own accountancy studies.

For many years, I had a physical connection with this shop. It was a table lamp that Stan had made from a turned wooden stand that used to support one of the glass shelves in the shop. This lamp stood on my desk throughout the years I was studying for my accountancy qualification. They did not have the shop for long. The accounts show that they rented it from the middle of December 1939 to the end of December 1940. Why did they give it up? Was trade poor due to so many people evacuating the town due to the risk of invasion?

When I wrote the first draft of this book, I worked on the assumption that the sweet business was established and largely run by Stan with little input from his brother, Jim. I was influenced in this assumption by how successfully Stan had run the business in the 1950s, which probably meant that it had always been run this way. However, further examination of old documents showed that Jim had been an important partner in the early business. I had Stan's old black metal bank deposit box that used to contain his important possessions and, in his lifetime, was kept at the Midland Bank in Westcliff. Inside the box was all his annual business accounts. The accounts for the early years show that Stan had put up some 53% of the business capital and that Jim had put up the remaining 47%. Also, both brothers were taking wages from the firm. So, the business started off as a true partnership of the two brothers.

An example of the sweets they sold is illustrated below in an extract from the day-book of 16th March 1937.

Sold to F H Marsh and Son, one quarter hundredweight (equivalent to 28 pounds or 12.7 kilograms) of each of:

Nut rock bars	9/- (nine shillings)
Nut rock	8/-
Cokernut toffee bars	9/-
Spearmint toffee	7/6 (seven shillings and six pence)
Nutty toffee	7/6
Treacle toffee	7/-
Black Jack toffee	7/-
Cokernut toffee	8/6
	Total £3/3/6

Payment is received by cheque on 19th March of £3/2/8, which is net of a 1¼% discount of ten pence.

(Note 'cokernut' is an antiquated word for 'coconut')

Leading up to World War II.

But what was going on in the wider world that would change Stan and Doris's lives so dramatically?

The end of the First World War in 1918 resulted in victory for the democratic countries of Britain, France and the United States. Germany was humiliated by defeat and was forced to pay large sums of money to the Allies for war damage. It lost most of its overseas possessions and was not allowed to build up its military forces. It became an unstable and demoralised country. In the 1920s, Germany suffered massive inflation and the collapse of its currency. As Winston Churchill said, 'the victors forget, the vanquished remember'. Germany was not going to forget its humiliation. Britain had a vast empire, France had many overseas possessions, and America was emerging as the world's greatest industrial power. The German people did not want the country to remain a second-class state, they wanted equal status with the Allied powers.

These were the conditions that allowed Hitler, a strong charismatic leader, and the Nazis to come to power. Although he had initially been democratically elected, Hitler quickly turned the country into a military dictatorship. The Nazis put the blame on the Jews for Germany's problems of previous decades. As a result, they became an increasingly persecuted group. As well as restoring the country's industrial power, Hitler set about building up its military capability. Queenie Cockshull, Doris's sister, observed at first hand the dominance that Hitler had over his people. Mick remembers Queenie telling him that in the late 1930s, when she was on holiday and staying in a hotel in Germany, she heard a commotion, went outside and saw Hitler passing in a car followed by goose-stepping soldiers. She understood from this how powerful the Nazis had become. (Goose-stepping soldiers kick their straight legs up in unison. George Orwell said, 'It is simply an affirmation of naked power; contained in it, quite consciously and intentionally, is the vision of a boot crashing down on a face'.) By 1938, Hitler had started his expansion of Germany by invading Austria then Czechoslovakia. But this was not enough, and in his quest for world domination, or as he put it 'more breathing space' for the German people, he invaded Poland on 1st September 1939. Britain had been slow to build up its military forces and was reluctant to challenge Germany's expansionist policies. However, Britain had a mutual defence pact with Poland and so, together with France, Britain declared war on Germany on 3rd September 1939.

Sam King must have been appalled that his family was to be put into great danger and a very uncertain future by yet another war with Germany. After all, he had fought in the Great War some twenty-five years earlier in order to bring peace to Britain and Europe. He had been an ambulance driver during the Battle of the Somme and, no doubt, had seen unimaginable carnage and suffering. His war ended with him being invalided out of the army in 1917 after contracting nephritis, a serious kidney infection. Politicians had said that World War One was the 'war to end all wars' and now German aggression was starting all over again.

3. 1939-40. Being bombed and getting married.

Defeats abroad, rationing at home, bombs from the air.

The war in the early months of 1940 did not go well for Britain and France. The news from abroad was desperate. Poland had already succumbed to a German invasion and in April Denmark surrendered and Norway was invaded. In May, Belgium, France, and the Netherlands fought losing battles trying to keep the German Army out of their countries.

In Britain basic foodstuffs were rationed in January 1940. By March, meat was also rationed as the Germans attacked food convoys in the Atlantic Ocean. (Little did Stan and Doris know then that rationing in some form would continue until the early 1950s.) Locally, German planes began dropping mines in the Thames to disrupt shipping, and all over England the German bombing of cities and ports began.

1939–40. BEING BOMBED AND GETTING MARRIED.

Map of Wartime Southend-on-Sea, Essex

Labels on map:
- Rochford R.A.F. Fighter Plane Aerodrome
- H Uncle Jim's Grave
- I New Factory 1946
- A127
- F 1946 House
- D Shop Sweet Factory
- E Parent's House
- A Stan/Doris House C
- B Bomb 333
- G Finchley Rd Bomb
- A13 Westcliff-on-Sea
- Southend-on-Sea
- H.M.S. Westcliff
- Southend Pier H.M.S. Leigh
- Tank Traps Along Seafront
- Shoebury Army Barracks
- Artillery Testing Ranges
- Anti Submarine Barrier
- River Thames

Southend-on-Sea Map – Key to places

A. 44 Mount Avenue, Westcliff-on-Sea, where Doris and Stan lived between 1940 and 1946.

B. Mount Avenue. The 333rd bomb of the 800 to be dropped on Southend Borough exploded here at 9.15 pm on 11th December 1940.

C. Sweet Factory in Shoe Lane. Stan and Jim started their business here in about 1937, and it continued to operate until 1946.

D. London Road sweet shop was only open for a year up to the end of 1940. It probably closed because so many people had evacuated the town.

E. Stan's parents, Samuel and Grace, and brother Jim's house at 63 Cotswold Road.

F. 305 Westborough Road. Doris arranged the purchase in time for Stan's return from the war in 1946.

G. Finchley Road. Four houses were destroyed by bombing on 10th October 1940, see the photograph in Chapter 3.

H. The family are buried in Sutton Road Cemetery. Jim, Samuel, Grace, Doris and Stan King.

I. The business moved to premises in Ely Road in 1946, and a new factory was built here in 1953. (Now a small housing estate.)

During World War II, Southend seafront was a naval area called HMS Westcliff and Southend Pier was another naval facility, known as HMS Leigh. The pier was a staging post for 3,367 wartime convoys, consisting of 84,297 ships. At Shoebury, to the east of the town, was an army barracks and artillery testing facility. To the north was RAF Rochford, a Spitfire and Hurricane fighter plane base.

What a perilous time to get married!

Doris did say that she and Stan wondered whether it was advisable to get married once the war had started, as the future was so uncertain. Millions of men had been killed in the First World War so there was no guarantee that Stan would survive another world war, and with the development of aerial bombing would Doris be any safer at home? But my mother told me they decided they wanted to take on the future risks together, so they married on the 9th June 1940. But what a perilous time they chose. Four weeks earlier, Winston Churchill had become Prime Minister and in his first speech to Parliament had promised to do everything in his power to achieve victory in the war. He said, 'I have nothing to offer but blood, toil, tears and sweat.' Words that from 2016 appear on every five-pound note.

1939-40. BEING BOMBED AND GETTING MARRIED.

By late May 1940, the German Army had occupied Holland, Belgium, and were moving into France. The British and French armies had just been driven back by the rapid German advance and were surrounded in northern Belgium. Six days before the wedding, the 'Miracle of Dunkirk' was completed when some 335,000 troops were hurriedly evacuated by a fleet of boats back to Britain from the beaches of Dunkirk. There was now a real risk of Hitler's troops invading Britain. On the 4th June Prime Minister Winston Churchill made his famous speech saying, 'We shall fight on the seas and oceans… in the air… we shall fight on the beaches… in the fields… in the streets… in the hills; we shall never surrender.' It was a stirring speech that inspired people to carry on the fight against Germany. But it also dramatically set out how close the country was to being invaded.

It is hard to imagine a more ominous background to the beginning of married life. Nevertheless, the wedding at a church in Forest Hill, South London was, judging by the happy faces in the photographs, a very happy occasion. Stan's brother, Jim, was best man and Doris's sister, Queenie, was the bridesmaid. Was the reason Doris did not wear a white wedding dress because the wedding was arranged in haste, or due to the scarcity of dress material, or because she wanted to make the dresses herself? In that period not all brides wore white wedding dresses. According to Wikipedia, 'British and American brides did not fully adopt the trend (for white wedding dresses) until after World War II.'

According to her sister, Queenie, Doris was skilled at dressmaking, which is demonstrated by the photograph (in Chapter 1) of a dress she made. My view is that she wanted to make the dress herself – she had the ability – and probably did so. I remember Doris saying that she was annoyed that, just as the wedding photographs were taken, the Church doors were noisily closed behind them. It must have been upsetting for Doris that her father was not well enough to give her away, as by this time it is believed he had been in a long-stay hospital for some years. She may have been given away by her uncle, David, or by her aunt's husband, Charles Butcher.

I expect she was pleased that the wedding was not interrupted by an air raid warning, or that the photographs did not have to be taken showing them carrying their gasmasks. The wedding reception photographs show the happy couple with their immediate family, Jim, Queenie and Doris's mother, Harriet, Uncle Charles and Auntie Dol (Harriet's sister). I remember Uncle Charles being a keen photographer, so perhaps he took the pictures. Whilst not in the photographs, Stan's parents, Sam and Grace, would have almost certainly been there. It is likely that the reception was held either in the garden of Doris's mother's shop or Stan's parents' house. With the wartime restrictions on travel, it would have been difficult for Stan's Cambridgeshire cousins to attend.

Married during the bombing of London. German air attacks were a regular feature of London life from May 1940. Stan and Doris's wedding took place on the 9th June 1940, at Forest Hill Church, South London. The best man was Stan's brother, Jim, and the bridesmaid was Doris's sister, Queenie. Doris kept a piece of her wedding bouquet as a memento, which was eventually passed down to Steve (which I still have).

The day after the wedding Italy declared war on Britain, and Norway surrendered to the Germans. Nine days after the wedding, and still feeling they were on their honeymoon, Stan and Doris heard on the BBC the report of another speech where Winston Churchill described 'the disastrous military events which have happened during the past fortnight' and warned of a German invasion. He went on to say 'The Battle of Britain is about to begin. Upon this battle depends our own British (way of) life… and the survival of Christian civilisation.' This must have sent a cold shiver down their spines. By the time Stan and Doris had finished their honeymoon (if they had one), all Britain's allies in Europe had been defeated; Britain was alone in fighting the now massive German empire. Even Ireland refused to help by not allowing Britain to use its ports as naval bases.

Two happy brothers and sisters at the reception after the wedding. In June 1940, Queenie Cockshull was thirty-five years old, Stan was twenty-eight, Doris was twenty-six and Jim King was thirty-one. Was this photo taken at the King family home, 8 Sylvan Grove, SE15 (with a sweet factory behind?) or at the rear of the Cockshull's shop at 163 Lordship Lane, SE22?

Invasion preparations, evacuation precautions, Spitfire heroics.

On 2nd July, Hitler ordered preparations for the invasion of Britain. But first he had to defeat the Royal Air Force so that his invasion force could land unhindered. The summer of 1940 saw one of the most dramatic and terrifying battles of the war, the 'Battle of Britain', and it all happened in the skies over the south east of England. The German air force, the Luftwaffe, sent hundreds of bomber and fighter planes day after day to try to bomb London and other cities into submission in what became known as the 'Blitz'.

Stan and Doris could look up and see the dogfights, as the outnumbered Spitfires and Hurricanes of the Royal Air Force attacked the German Messerschmitt fighters that were escorting the bombers. The Germans tried to obliterate the Royal Air Force (RAF) by bombing their airfields, so that they would have mastery of the skies. Stan and Doris, now living in Westcliff-on-Sea, found themselves living in an invasion risk area. Southend became a restricted coastal zone and a defence area and only residents or those with official permits were allowed entry. Restrictions were strict, for example bus passengers were warned that there would be no refund of their fare if they were ejected from the bus for not having an official pass!

Stan had brought his bride to live in a town that could be invaded by the Germans at any time. Twelve days after the wedding, notices were displayed all over Southend (according to Dee Gordon's book *Southend at War*) proclaiming:

'You Should Take Precautions Now To Ensure That You Could Leave At Short Notice.'

In preparation for an invasion, the local wartime regulation told residents to keep a suitcase packed, as they would only have one hour to get to a Southend railway station in order to escape the fighting, when the invasion came. As a result of these dire warnings, some 84,000 residents left Southend within the next few weeks. Sam and Grace (who it is believed had also moved to Southend by this time), together with Stan and Doris, were amongst some of the only 15,500 civilians left in the town. It must have been very worrying to know that most of your neighbours had fled. Why did they stay in the town? There could have been several reasons. They had no children that they needed to protect, they had a business they wanted to keep running, they did not want to leave their factory unattended, or perhaps, most significantly, they were one of the few people with a motor vehicle so could escape quickly. Nevertheless, did they make some informal arrangements to join Stan's cousins in Cambridgeshire should the German Army land on the nearby beaches?

Stan and Jim had rented a shop at 505 London Road, almost opposite their factory, in December 1939. Was the reason they closed the shop after one year because so many people had left the town?

Still the bad news continued. On 30th June 1940, the Channel Islands were invaded. And two weeks later, Hitler declared a blockade of Britain in order to try to starve Britain into surrender. At the beginning of August, Hitler set 15th September as the date for 'Operation Sea Lion', the code name for the invasion of Britain. Towards the end of August, the bombing 'Blitz' on London intensified. By the 7th September, there were 2,000 dead in London.

In the same month there were heavy losses of shipping in the Atlantic due to attacks by German 'U- boat' submarines. However, the RAF held the Luftwaffe at bay. Britain's aircraft factories had been able to replace damaged aircraft much more quickly than the Germans had envisaged. Fighter station runways were quickly repaired. The Spitfires and Hurricanes proved more than a match for the German aircraft and pilot numbers were swelled by Empire and Polish volunteers. As a result, by 15th September, Hitler's attempt to obliterate British airpower had failed. The 'Battle of Britain' had been won, although this did not stop the continued bombing of British cities. For example, on 14th November, Coventry Cathedral was set ablaze in a massive fire-bombing raid and the medieval centre of the city destroyed. Stan said that Churchill's stirring speeches 'got them through the war' and he must have been moved by the Prime Minister's appreciation of the valour of the pilots of the RAF when he referred to them by saying, 'Never in the course of human history have so many owed so much to so few.'

The report of a bombing raid on Southend-on-Sea on 10th October 1940. The main picture shows the destruction of four houses in Finchley Road, not far from Stan's sweet factory and his parents' house. The newspaper report was heavily censored as it only refers to bombs being dropped on 'a South East Town'. Many newspaper readers, however, would have known where this was, as I expect news of bombing raids spread quickly through the town. (These houses were just opposite 20 Finchley Road, where Doris's sister, Queenie, and her mother were to live after the war.)

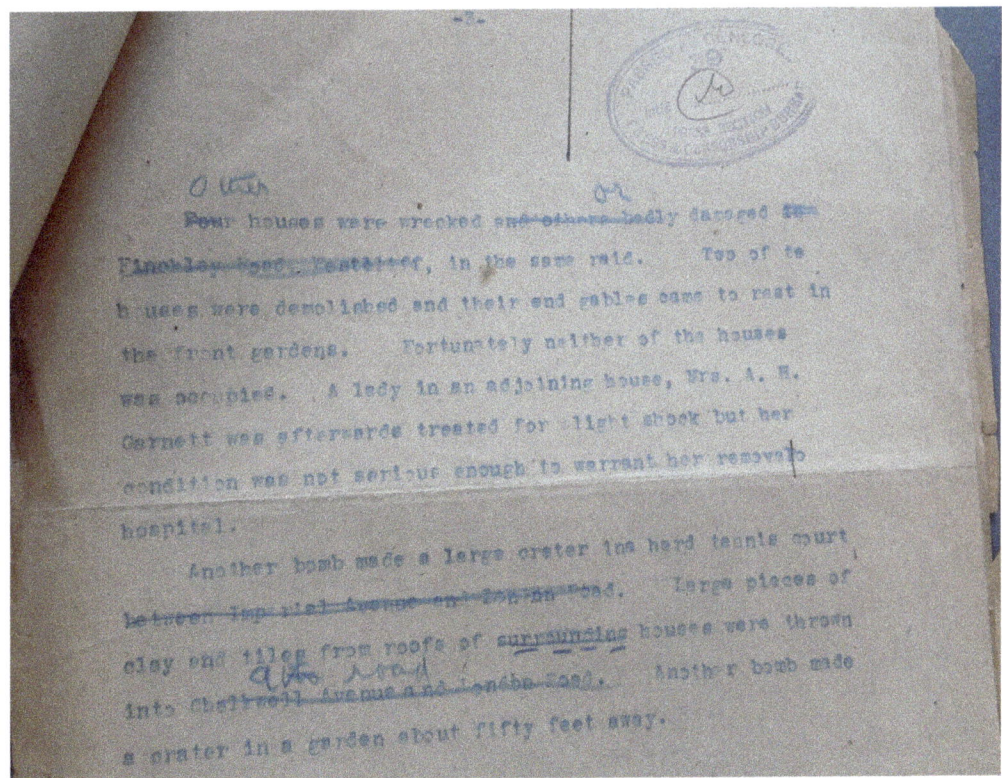

Southend Pictorial reporter's original draft report of the bombing of houses in Finchley Road (see previous photo). The typed report has been 'blue lined' (censored) by the official censor to avoid giving any specific information that may be useful to the enemy.

Bride 'On the Front Line'.

It is said that a woman remains a bride up to her first wedding anniversary. During that year she still lives in the glow of a glorious wedding, she enjoys becoming independent of the parental home and starts homemaking herself and can revel in the excitement and novelty of living with the man of her life. But was it like this for Doris? There is no doubt, I feel, that Doris and Stan were very much in love and, as they say, 'love conquers all'. But Doris was living in a war zone, with a potential German invasion beach only half a mile away and had been told by the authorities to have a suitcase packed in case the call came in for an emergency evacuation.

There was no pleasure in living in a seaside town in wartime. The beach was out of bounds to civilians, and even if access had been allowed, it was covered in obstacles to prevent enemy landing craft coming ashore. The wartime photograph of the seafront (shown at the end of Chapter 5) shows some of the 1,000 large concrete blocks placed along the foreshore (two of which remain to this day near the old gas works pier on Eastern Esplanade) to prevent enemy tanks entering the town. There were anti-aircraft gun positions in many places. I remember the remains of one on the sundeck of Westcliff swimming pool when I used to go swimming there in the early 1960s. Stan said that the Southend Arterial Road was littered with obstacles, such as oil barrels, so that you had to drive in a zigzag fashion along it. This was to prevent the road being used as a landing runway for German invasion aircraft. Doris said that one of the houses they had looked at with a view to renting (near Hamlet Court Road, Westcliff-on-Sea) was later destroyed by bombing and how lucky they were not to have moved there.

Did Doris ever have second thoughts about whether Southend was a good location to set up home at the start of her married life? Or did she just accept the hardships of war as everyone else had to? As well as all the depressing news on the BBC radio, she was to get another shock closer to home.

After their marriage, Stan and Doris rented a house, number 44 Mount Avenue, in a very pleasant part of Westcliff-on-Sea. It was a modern detached house halfway down a hill leading to Chalkwell Station and with a view of the River Thames. It is still a very attractive street today. The rent was probably very reasonable, due to so many people having evacuated the town. And people had good reason to find a safer part of the country to live as, on average during 1940, one high explosive bomb dropped every day somewhere in Southend. The sound of explosions was a part of everyday life for Doris and Stan.

The evening of 11th December 1940 probably began in the usual way of Stan arriving home, washing the sweet factory cornflour from his hands and face, listening to the news on the radio and having dinner with Doris. However, it was cruelly disturbed when at 9.15 a bomb, the 333rd to land on Southend, full of 50 kg of high explosives, landed in their street not far from their home. Did they have time to get to an air raid shelter? Was the house damaged? Were they personally affected by the blast? We know from the wartime bomb records that no one was killed or injured. But why, after such a dramatic incident in their lives, did Doris and Stan never mention this event to their children?

Southend, being at the mouth of the Thames, was on the route that German bombers took when attacking London. So, it was very convenient to drop bombs on the way to London or on the way home if they had some left over. Also, there was a military barracks in the east of the town at Shoeburyness, an RAF base just over the Borough boundary in Rochford and a naval base, H.M.S Westcliff, on the seafront. The town was therefore an enemy target in its own right. In the first year of Luftwaffe attacks, six men, nine women and one child had been killed and eighty-eight people injured as a result of the bombing raids on the town. Despite the bombing, many people who had evacuated the town in the summer began to return to Southend by the end of 1940 as the risk of invasion diminished, although many evacuated children did not return to the town until much later.

Southend Police Station in Alexandra Street surrounded by sandbags to diffuse bomb shrapnel. Ordinary houses were rarely protected. The building in the foreground, 29 Alexandra Street, still exists and is where my brother Michael started work in 1960 and I was interviewed for a job with Southend Council in 1963. The Police Station site is now a car park.
Another building that was protected was Westminster College in Westminster Drive, where I went to school between 1953 and 1959. There was a brick bench in front of the windows at the back of the school. I was told that during the war this was the base of a wall that rose to cover the lower windows in order to protect the young pupils during air raids.

4. 1941. White aprons and humbugs, to khaki and engines.

The War in 1941 – could it get any worse?

Heavy German bombing raids on London and other British cities continued in the early months of 1941. Important buildings were hit. On 11th January, the Bank of England was damaged, and the adjacent underground station destroyed. On 8th March, Buckingham Palace was hit, and on 19th April, while St Paul's was only slightly damaged, other churches built by Sir Christopher Wren in the 17th century were destroyed. The following day 223,000 Greek soldiers surrendered to the Germans and Britain began to evacuate its forces from Greece. On 24th April the British battle cruiser HMS Hood was sunk by the German battleship Bismarck, which days later was itself sunk following an attack by planes from the carrier HMS Ark Royal. The German navy had its revenge in November when the Ark Royal was sunk by a U-boat. (My sister-in-law, Dionne's, uncle-in-law, Bob Clark, was among the 1,415 sailors killed on HMS Hood.) In June, Hitler invaded Russia and by October German troops were approaching Moscow. And, in December 1941, there was a surprise Japanese attack on the American Pacific Fleet at Pearl Harbour, Hawaii, which brought the United States into the war. On Christmas Day, British Hong Kong fell to the Japanese. So, a year of depressing news, although at last Britain had two allies in Russia and America.

A near miss. My aunt, Queenie, explained to me that this was bomb damage near her mother's shop at 163 Lordship Lane, Dulwich. It reminded her how lucky she was to escape injury during the war.

Confectioner to soldier.

Like many men, I suspect Stan wanted to do his duty to help protect his homeland, yet it would have been fully understandable if he had doubts about wanting to join the army. If you were, say, eighteen, the thought of joining the army and shooting a few Germans would be exciting. However, by 1941, Stan was of the mature age of thirty. Also, he knew all about the horrors of the trenches in the First World War from the stories told by his father. Samuel had been injured at the Battle of the Somme in 1916 and invalided out of that conflict (according to his war record). More practically, he had moved to Southend not long before the war to start his own sweet confectionery business and wanted to establish this. Most importantly of all, he had met the love of his life, Doris, and married her in the summer of 1940 and would naturally want to be with her when they started a family. However, Britain was in a 'life and death' struggle with Germany, and there was a sense that everyone in the country was pulling together for the common good and Stan would have wanted to have played his part.

In April 1939, the Military Training Act required all young fit men to register to join the army; this was extended on September 6th to all men between the ages of eighteen and forty. In 1941, the upper age limit was increased to fifty-one, although few older men were called up, and women also became liable for military service. By the end of 1940, 4.1m had registered and 2.2m were called up in 1941. By April 1945, some 5m men, a third of the entire male population, were in the armed forces – 3m in the army.

Stan was not in the initial compulsory 'call up', but he decided to do something to help the war effort. Motor cars were in the blood of the King family. Stan's grandfather was one of the first to own a 'new-fangled' motor car in 1902 and Stan's dad had queued up for a driving licence on the first day they were issued in 1903, and he had a job as a chauffeur. So, it was no surprise that as a young man Stan wanted to get involved with automobiles and managed to get a job as an apprentice and qualify as a motor mechanic, although the great depression of the early 1930s had closed off that as a career. So, Stan decided to leave his fledgling sweet business in the hands of his father and Doris and to put his mechanical expertise to good use by taking a job at the Ford Dagenham motor plant on war work. This job enabled him to stay living at home and he probably hoped that he would be in a 'protected occupation', which would exempt him from the 'call up'. However, that was not to be the case as, on August 7th 1941, he enlisted in the army at Cambridge. He probably enlisted there in the hope that his Cambridge cousins might be in the same regiment.

By this time, Doris, whether she knew it or not, was already one month pregnant.

What did Stan do in the army?

As Stan had spoken very little about what he did during his four and a half years in the army, I had to try and find out. Fortunately, I had his army pay-book, which told me he was in the Royal Army Service Corps (RASC) and gave some clues as to which company he was in. In 2011, I applied to the Army Personnel Office in Glasgow for a copy of his war record. It arrived a year later! And while it showed details of his training courses and leave, it explained little of what he did. Research at the Army Museum in Chelsea was fruitless, except for the discovery that there was a RASC regimental museum in Camberley, Surrey. This was my next stop. Fortunately, the museum was quiet when I visited and the curator was able to spend most of the afternoon helping me. He explained that there were some 900 companies but, from the information I gave him, he was almost certain that Stan served with 486 Company. (This was confirmed when, a couple of years later, I noticed a reference to 486 Company on Stan's only letter home that has survived.)

The curator very helpfully provided me with an electronic copy of the history of the regiment. In this book there were chapters on the role of about half a dozen of the many companies. As luck would have it, Stan's 486 Company was one of those described in detail. Having identified his company, I now visited the National Records Office at Kew and read through the war reports that his company headquarters were required to return to the War Office on a daily basis. Despite the fact that the war reports were marked 'Confidential until 2045', I was able to read and photograph them. They made fascinating reading and provided a definitive record of where his company travelled.

His company consisted of some 395 men (according to the 29th July 1944 field return) split into four platoons, a headquarters and workshop group. These platoons/groups were often located up to one hundred miles apart. So, as I did not know at the time which group Stan was attached to, I could not precisely track the route he took in the war. It was not until early 2014, when I re-read the only surviving letter he sent to Doris (see Chapter 6) that I noticed that his address at the top of the page included the letters 'w/s'. I should have realised from his mechanical expertise that this signified he was in the 'workshop' group. I could now identify him to a group of probably some 50 men amongst an army of some four million.

Early army life and good news from home.

Soldiers often comment that the transition from the freedoms of civilian life to the discipline and regimentation of military life is difficult, and Stan may have found it no different. There was no doubt that the war was necessary, pretty well everyone agreed on that. The Nazis were ruthless, and Britain would be defeated and invaded unless everyone played their part in the war effort. It is doubtful if Stan had any say as to which part of the armed forces he was attached to. He was an experienced driver, like his father in the First World War, and a mechanic, so putting him in the army's main transport service, the Royal Army Service Corps, was entirely logical. (Was Stan put in the RASC because his father Samuel, on enlisting on 2nd December 1914, had also joined the Army Service Corps-Mechanical Transport?)

The day after enlisting, he joined A Company in Blackburn, Lancashire. Here he would have to learn the discipline of a soldier's life: early morning marching up and down, or 'square bashing', on the parade ground; being shouted at by the sergeant major; having to clean his kit in fastidious detail and learning to use his rifle. He once explained how gruelling the ten-mile hikes 'at the double' were, weighed down with full kit, and he remembered the marks the heavy strapping left on his body. The *WW2Talk* website explains that all RASC soldiers are trained to fight as infantry, so could be called upon to be in the front line of battle if necessary.

It must have seemed a long two months up to his first home leave of seven days in mid-October 1941. The best part of one day would have been spent travelling up from Boscombe, Hampshire, where he was now stationed, and a similar time travelling back, so it was closer to only five days with his wife. Doris was now two months pregnant, but did she realise it? After all, sex education was non-existent in those days and it was not till many years later that pregnancy testing kits were available. Also, advice was hard to come by as pre-natal medical staff had been evacuated from Southend due to its hospital being used mainly for military personnel. Nevertheless, if she did realise, Doris could at last tell Stan he was to become a father and also talk about her pregnancy and the changes it would make to their family life.

On his way back to his army base at Boscombe, Stan must have felt elated and overjoyed by Doris's news that they were to be starting a family. His army service was going well and he was now categorised as a Classified Driver Class III. Another treasured seven days' leave was granted in November. He was now with the No1 RASC Training Battalion and he transferred to Bulford, Wiltshire, for a fitter's course and at Canterbury he passed a motor mechanics course.

Stan said he really enjoyed the mechanics courses. In later years, he liked telling the story of one of the fault-finding exercises set by the instructors. He was set the task of finding out why a particular lorry engine would not start. He checked all the obvious things (e.g. lack of petrol, no spark at the plugs, inaccurate timing, dodgy starter motor), but there was nothing amiss and he conceded defeat. The instructors then showed him the large hole they had drilled in the induction tract. He always looked for the unexpected after that.

Doris and Stan must have been really looking forward to the next leave home, as this would be the last time they could spend alone as a couple before years of family life.

However, the prospect of a few idyllic days at home together was transformed by events near Sheffield.

5. 1942-43. The joy of parenthood and the tragedy of war.

A unique tragedy – the Beighton Train Disaster.

James Samuel King was Stan's elder brother by two years and was living with his parents in Southend in the early part of the war. (I recall my grandparents referring to one of the bedrooms in their house in 63 Cotswold Road, Westcliff as 'Jim's room'.) I remember my father mentioning that Jim had trained to be, or was in training to be, a draughtsman or architect (one of my prize possessions is his technical ruler and geometry set). He was probably working with Stan in the confectionery business in Southend just before hostilities started. Not too much is known about Jim, although my grandparents once mentioned that he had been in a motorcycle accident, resulting in it landing in a ditch on top of him, which apparently left him with a limp thereafter.

Jim was a gunner in the Royal Artillery. He was probably selected for that role due to his knowledge of draftsmanship, as mathematics and geometry would have been useful in the aiming and trajectory of gunshot. Or it could have been that Jim just joined the local military as it is known that the Royal Artillery was stationed at Shoeburyness Barracks.

In February 1942 Jim's sister-in-law, Doris, was living alone in Westcliff and no doubt missing her husband during her first pregnancy. Her sister and mother were still living in Dulwich. Stan, who had not seen his wife since November and his brother for probably many months more, was on a fitter's course in Bulford, Wiltshire. Mother, Grace, and father, Sam, were in Westcliff and helping to keep the sweet business running in preparation for both their sons' return after the war.

1942-43. THE JOY OF PARENTHOOD AND THE TRAGEDY OF WAR.

It is likely that on Friday 13th February 1942 a policeman from the central police station in Alexandria Street rode on his bicycle to 63 Cotswold Road to tell Sam and Grace the terrible news that their eldest son had been killed. It is hard to imagine the shock, distress and disbelief that this knock on the door caused. They must have found it very difficult to break the news to the heavily pregnant Doris in case the shock caused complications. How could this tragedy happen when Jim was not even in a war zone? It emerged that Jim was very unlucky to have been involved in one of the most unusual fatalities of the war.

I knew from listening to brief conversations between my father and grandfather that my uncle Jim had been killed in a train crash during the war, but I knew nothing of the circumstances. I started investigating the crash in 2013 and came across an internet post from Chris Hobbs, a reporter on a Sheffield newspaper, who had been investigating the crash. I contacted Chris who gave me much information and supplied me with contacts to other people who had an interest in the disaster. Chris Hobbs now has a website with a section on the crash. The following is a summary of what happened.

On Wednesday 11th February 1942, 170 sailors boarded a troop train at Chatham, Kent. They were to travel to the Clyde in Scotland to join a new destroyer, HMS Partridge. The train stopped in Woolwich to take on 190 officers and men, including James King, mainly from the Royal Artillery. They were to join troop ships to take them overseas. Their destination could have been the Far East as Malaya was under attack from the Japanese and Singapore fell four days after Jim boarded that fateful troop train.

At 3.30am on 11th February, a goods train left Frodingham for West Tinsley, near Sheffield. Amongst the wagons it was pulling was one loaded three days before by the 'experienced men' of the Appleby-Frodingham Steel Company and passed for safety by an examiner. On the wagon was a one and a quarter ton steel plate. After dropping off other wagons, the train arrived at Holbrook Colliery Sidings at 8.15 pm. There were three sidings (short railway tracks with bumpers at the end used to park wagons) at Holbrook and it was necessary to manoeuvre wagons into the correct sidings.

A railway guard called Calladine was acting as shunter (driver of a small locomotive used to move wagons), while a guard named Helliwell was responsible for controlling the wagons into the sidings. Several shunts were made until only two wagons were attached to the engine. Calladine released the plate wagon and Helliwell was waiting for it some sixty yards away down a 1 in 165 slope. The wagon was 'loose shunted' (i.e. it rolled down the slope until it made contact with other wagons in the siding). Neither Calladine nor Helliwell heard anything unusual as it made contact. It appears that it was at this crucial moment that the steel plate moved and projected over the side of the wagon. Crucially, the siding was adjacent to the main line and the steel plate was overhanging towards it.

Guard Helliwell travelled back down the main line on the footplate past the plate wagon but in the darkness saw nothing amiss. Calladine made a tour of the yard but had no occasion to pass along the somewhat narrow space between the plate wagon and the main line. Had either guard spotted that the steel plate had moved and was now overhanging the main line the ensuing tragedy would have been avoided. Similarly, had the shunting engine or the goods train that came down the main line at 9.23 pm hit the protruding plate the alarm would have been raised.

The scene was now set for tragic consequences. An extract from the BBC's *WW2 People's War* explains:

'The night was fine but dark and there was a sharp frost as, at 9.56, the Glasgow bound troop train travelling at about 35 mph, and under clear signals, ran down the incline towards Beighton Station. As the train passed the protruding plate, the locomotive, being marginally narrower than the coaching stock, missed it. However, some of the handles on the first and second coaches made contact with it. The third coach, being three inches narrower, evaded the obstacle, but the fourth one struck the corner of the plate halfway along its side causing it to rotate further and cut more deeply into the fifth. The plate then embedded itself into the side of the sixth coach to a maximum depth of six feet… On the troop train, the driver, fireman and a guard had no indication that anything was untoward until a damaged vacuum pipe automatically brought the train to a standstill. On board the train, a strange situation ensued with many in the front and rear coaches unaware that anything was amiss, but in the centre portion it was a scene of chaos and carnage. Eleven soldiers had been killed, nearly forty badly injured and many more were trapped inside the wreckage… Roused by the sound of the crash… Stationmaster Edgar Allan rapidly formed rescue parties. Among the first to arrive was a group of miners who were returning from nearby Waleswood Colliery on the pit bus… For the first few minutes, everyone toiled in total darkness, but limited illumination was soon forthcoming. The spectacle was a grim one as rescuers fought to save lives amid the dim light provided by torches and lamps.

'More assistance arrived as members of the local St John's Ambulance Brigade, Red Cross, Home Guard, A.R.P. and Civil Defence began to work tirelessly throughout the night. Two local GPs, Dr De Dombal from Beighton and Dr G.R. Lipp from Killamarsh, worked magnificently throughout the night, assisted by first aid parties and, eventually, doctors and nurses from Sheffield and Chesterfield… Fourteen soldiers lost their lives and thirty-five others were severely injured. Eleven of the dead were taken to the station waiting room, which served as a temporary mortuary, whilst the other unfortunate servicemen died on their way to or at Sheffield Royal Infirmary.'

The Commonwealth War Graves website shows most fatalities occurred on 11th February; however, two are recorded as dying on 12th February, including James King. So, it seems he survived to be taken to Sheffield Royal Infirmary.

I remember in the 1950s/1960s regular visits to Jim's grave with Sam, Grace, Stan and Doris. Mick, John and I knew a little of what had happened to our uncle. Although I remember being shocked on one occasion when Sam commented that some of the soldiers had been beheaded in the train crash. It was clearly an awful memory for the family.

So, who or what was to blame for the crash? There were three factors. Firstly, Guard Helliwell should have braked the plate wagon to slow it down as it rolled down to the end of the siding. The Inspecting Officer for the Ministry of War Transport commented that 'Responsibility for the incident rests with Helliwell', although he hesitated to criticise him unduly for his failure to apply the brake, he felt that a younger and more active man would have checked the wagon. Secondly, the clearance between the siding and the main line was not in accordance with modern practice and had there been the full nine feet, the incident would not have occurred. Thirdly, the method of transporting large metal sheets was fraught with danger and was changed after this incident. (Was the Inspecting Officer right to place responsibility for the accident on one person in view of the other factors that contributed to the tragedy?)

Sixty-four years later, in 2006, and with the memory of the accident still clear in her mind, an eyewitness to the tragedy, Eileen Hayward, submitted this account to the *BBC's People's War* website.

'Phyllis Simms and I were on a [Air Raid Precaution] roster, when an alert call came in: "Proceed to Beighton". We drove on half-masked side lights through the blackout; our guess was that it was a pit disaster. How wrong we were! The police directed us to the railway station. The incident was down on the rail tracks and we had a walk of 200 yards. A 2-cwt steel plate protruding from a goods train had cut through the carriages… Many service personnel were injured or dying; they had been sitting by the window asleep, reading or playing cards. Miners coming off work from Waleswood Colliery helped us with the stretcher cases.

'A young soldier I was attending told the sailor who had come to help me, "the navy is too late this time," and died a few seconds later. Phyllis and I arrived back at the station, black with dirt and very tired at 5.35 hours.'

The aftermath of the Beighton Train Disaster, showing the damaged carriages. This is the only photograph of the accident that I have been able to find.

Stan was informed of the death of his brother, but it was over a month later before he was allowed leave from the army in order to share the family grief with his wife, now eight months pregnant, and his parents.

Having to deal with family tragedy, separation from loved ones and the risks from enemy bombing, together with food rationing and an uncertain financial future, must have been very stressful. It is no wonder that Stan said that the reason he and Doris got into the regular smoking habit was the worry of the war.

TROOP TRAIN ACCIDENT NEAR SHEFFIELD

14 · Dead and 36 Injured

An accident to a troop train just outside Beighton Station, near Sheffield, late on Wednesday night caused 14 deaths and injuries to 36 men.

It is understood that the accident was caused by a piece of sheet steel which projected from a stationary goods train. The sides of carriages were ripped out and soldiers and sailors were thrown on to the rail track. The damaged coaches did not leave the line, but the torn-off doors with other wreckage lay on the track amid a litter of steel helmets, respirators, and other equipment.

Miners and villagers, first in darkness and then by the flickering light of hand-lamps, helped to drag dead and injured Service men from the wreckage.

Rescue work went on for four hours. The injured were rushed to Sheffield hospitals in ambulances, which with doctors and nurses were soon on the scene.

"The injured were mostly trapped in loose wreckage," said Mr. Charles Booth, a colliery ambulance instructor, who took a team of seven men with blankets and stretchers to the spot. The scene at the station was described as "like a shambles."

Soldiers in the first half of the train were most seriously involved. As they were taken from the wreckage villagers comforted them before they were hurried to hospital.

"There was not a word of complaint from any of the injured," said a rescuer. "One man was upset because he had just written to his wife telling her he was all right. He was afraid she would worry on hearing of the crash. Another man was anxious about his rosary."

One man probably owes his life to the fact that a comrade was thrown on top of him.

The names of two of the dead who died on the way to Sheffield are given as Ernest Rodgers, of Woolwich, and Amos Albert Hollingsworth, of Beeston, both Army men. A third, Samuel King, of Cotswold Street, Westcliffe-on-Sea, died in Sheffield Royal Hospital.

Breakdown gangs had cleared the line by dawn.

Could Jim have been saved? This report indicates that Jim was the only one of the fatally injured soldiers to still be alive upon reaching Sheffield Royal Hospital. Could modern medical trauma facilities have saved his life? This Manchester Guardian report of 13th April 1942 is some two months after the accident, an indication of how careful the press and the authorities were not to damage public morale or give any military information, in this case about troop movements, that might help the enemy. Note that Jim's middle name has been used in the report.

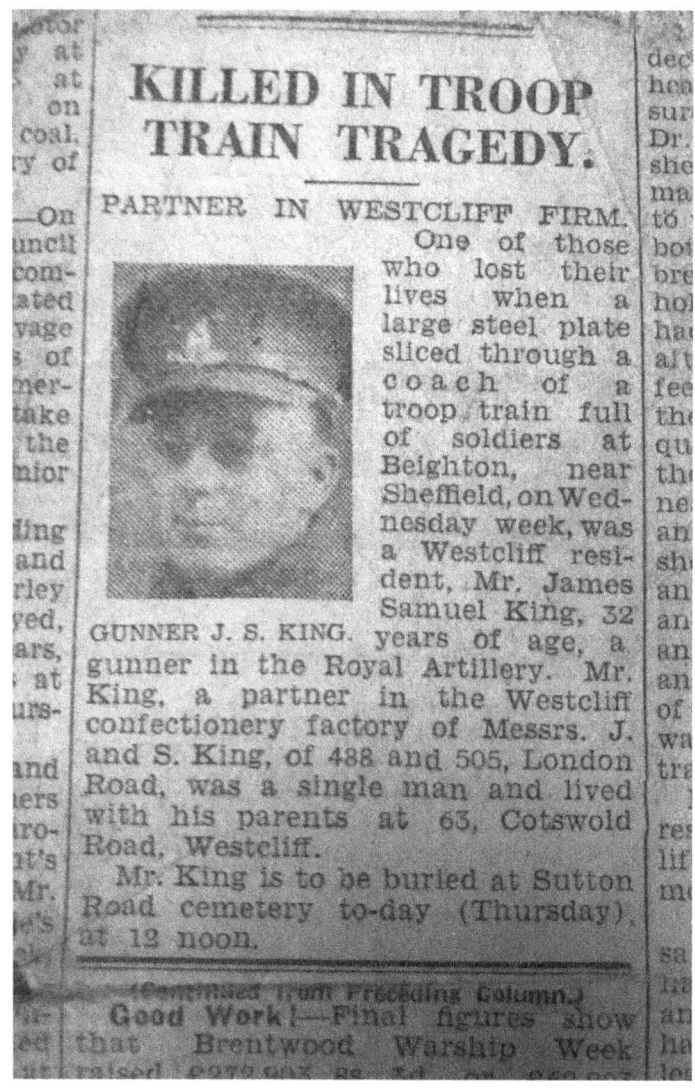

A cutting from the Southend Standard newspaper from 19th February 1942 that Jim's parents preserved. The local papers were apparently able to report the tragedy more quickly than the national papers. Although Stan was not far away (in Canterbury, Kent, on a motor mechanics course), he was unable to get leave from the army to attend his brother's funeral.

Stan's parents, Samuel and Grace, at their son, Jim's, grave in Sutton Road Cemetery, Southend in the late 1950s. I remember visits of the whole family several times a year to Jim's grave. In the background are the Commonwealth War Graves Commission gravestones, and the official memorial for the Southend war dead. Jim was buried outside the Commission's burial plot as his was a private internment. This enabled his family to have a more substantial memorial.

Joy after sadness.

After the terrible family bereavement in February, Doris had only four weeks to wait for the birth of her first child.

Childbirth is never without its risks. The wartime shortages of medics and medicines made the possibility that complications would be inadequately handled much greater. A distressing example of this occurred just over a year earlier in north London. On the 8th November each year my wife remembers her only sister. In 1940, Mary's mother, Vera, was admitted to a nursing home in Enfield to have her first child. Beds in hospitals were in short supply at that time, due to the high number of military casualties and the shortage of doctors. The baby girl died just after being born, a devastating event for any family. In peacetime she may have survived. Vera and her husband, John, probably decided not to risk having another child in wartime conditions. This may have meant that they could not have children at all because by the end of the war Vera was forty-three years old and may have been too old to conceive. Fortunately, this was not the case and Mary was born the year after the war finished. However, the earlier child is never forgotten.

In early 1942, Southend was a restricted area with a large military presence. There was an army barracks to the east of the town, an RAF aerodrome to the north and a naval presence on the sea front. In the Thames Estuary, naval and military casualties were routinely arriving from combat zones. Royal Navy ships regularly docked at the end of Southend Pier and transferred their wounded to local hospitals for treatment. To make space for this stream of military casualties, Southend General Hospital and Rochford Hospital (maternity and obstetrics) were partially emptied of local resident patients. As a result, there were almost no facilities for maternity care for local women. As Doris was still living in Southend during her pregnancy, she must have found it very difficult to get any pre-natal care. She did not have any close relatives who had had babies with whom she could have learned from. Today, from books and the internet, there is a mass of information available about having babies, as well as a superb National Health Service. But it was not like this in 1942. Doris once confided in me that she was almost completely ignorant about childbirth before her first child was born and had little idea what was going to happen to her.

The lack of local facilities meant that Doris had to travel elsewhere to have her baby. Early in April 1942, she travelled by train with her sister, Queenie, to Woking, in Surrey, to have her first baby. Queenie told me that she took time off from work in London to be with Doris. And on 15th April John Stanley King was born. At that period mothers were required to stay in hospital for twelve days after giving birth. Stan was on a course in London in early April and must have thought he could arrange to see Doris when she arrived in nearby Woking to have the baby. However, according to his war record, he was unable to obtain leave. Then, four weeks after John was born, Stan was transferred to the other end of the country to Paisley, in Scotland.

There was no chance of a twenty-four-hour pass from there to see his wife and new son! Although perhaps the army did have a heart after all because on 18th May he was transferred to Woking, where a month earlier Doris had given birth. This was unfortunate timing by the army as Doris would, most likely, have travelled back to Southend by then. However, the army did give Stan two weeks' leave from 20th May, so he saw his son for the first time when he was five weeks old.

Once Stan rejoined his army unit, Doris was left to care for her baby largely on her own, as it is believed her mother and sister were still living in Dulwich at that time, although her in-laws were only a couple of miles away.

Doris was not a superstitious person, so it seemed a little out of character when she told me that she went to a fortune teller before the war. The fortune teller read her palm and told her that she would have three sons. The prediction had started correctly, and she was amused that the fortune teller was to be proved accurate.

News from the various war fronts was desperate. In February, in the Far East, the British garrison in Singapore surrendered to the Japanese. In Britain the electricity, coal and gas and clothing ration was again decreased. In one of the worst naval disasters of the war, Convoy PQ17 sailed from Iceland in June with vital food and military supplies for Russia. The convoy was attacked by German U-boats and planes and twenty-four of the thirty-five merchant ships were sunk.

No better way to cheer up Stan after the death of his brother. Doris and Stan's firstborn son, John, at three months.

Stan gets home leave for the Christening of John in May 1942. Doris wears the hat she wore at her wedding. Outside 44 Mount Avenue, Westcliff-on-Sea.

Back into uniform and carrying full army kit, minus his gun, Stan goes back to the war after John's Christening.

1942-43. THE JOY OF PARENTHOOD AND THE TRAGEDY OF WAR.

Invasion training, home alone, and pregnant.

Many companies of the RASC were being sent abroad to support British Army units fighting the Italians and Germans in North Africa and the Japanese advancing towards India. Stan was fortunate not to be sent to join them. It was probably because he had not finished his mechanic and fitter training that he was kept in England.

More training courses followed. In early May 1942 he passed the motor vehicle fitters class III course in London. He was then taken on the strength of Company 6 Holding Brigade RASC in Paisley, Scotland. However, five days later he was with No 1 Holding Battalion in Woking, Surrey. The following month he underwent gas chamber training.

Gas attacks had proved lethal during the First World War. Chlorine was first used by the Germans at the Second Battle of Ypres in April 1915 and there was always the fear the Germans might use this weapon again in the Second World War. As a result, soldiers had to undergo training for such an attack. The training probably involved going through a gas filled room wearing their gas masks. There were also fears that British streets would be subject to gas attacks from German aeroplanes. The government responded to this threat by issuing all adults and children with gasmasks. By the beginning of the war, some thirty-eight million had been distributed. In May 1940 an additional filter was added to gas masks to protect against Arsine gases. Civilians were always asked to carry their gas masks. However, as early as 1941 national newspapers were reporting that the majority of adults did not bother to carry their gas masks. Fortunately, they never needed to be used.

By June 1942 Stan was with the 31st Tank Brigade in Swindon. He was awarded two valuable days' leave in August and was able to see his four-month-old son for the first time in three months and was given another seven days leave in September 1942. By November he was at the Motor Fitters School in Aldershot and was promoted to Fitter Class II. In the same month there was the first positive battlefield news of the war.

General Montgomery's Eighth Army defeated General Rommel's Afrika Korps at the Battle of El Alamein in North Africa. This prevented the Germans capturing Egypt and the Suez Canal and gaining access to the vital Middle East oilfields. There was still more training for Stan and he took a fitter's exam in January 1943. He passed and was awarded nine days' leave. In February 1943 he was with the 16th Tank Brigade RASC at Linton and was then transferred back to Aldershot. In June he passed the standard Trade Test and was upgraded to Fitter Group A Class I. It was then back to Linton with the 16th Tank Brigade Company RASC, with which he stayed until May 1944.

A short break from army training and manoeuvres sees Stan able to play with John, then probably fifteen months old, in the summer of 1943.

In July 1943 he was promoted to acting Lance Corporal, in December to acting Corporal, and in March 1944 to the full rank of Corporal, with a slight increase in pay. Stan got a week's leave in each of April, July and October 1943. This was his best year for leave in the army. Little did he know it, but he would not see much of Doris and his family for the next two years.

From November 1943 his location is recorded in his army records as 'Home', meaning 'home country' not Southend! There was to be no opening of presents with Doris and twenty-month-old John at Christmas 1943 as, for the third year running, Christmas is spent on duty with the army. He does, however, get nine days' leave in January 1944. It is on this leave that Doris can celebrate with Stan that she is now three months pregnant. How they must have both looked forward to the nine days' leave that Stan applied for in April 1944, so they could enjoy John's second birthday together and plan for another baby. And how disappointed they must have been when the leave was cancelled. Were they aware of the momentous events that were being planned in great secrecy for June 1944? And did they anticipate then that they would have to be apart for another sixteen months?

Stan does not appear in military records again until 15th May 1944, where he is listed with 'X list 51st Reserve Holding Unit'.

A rare photograph of Southend Promenade, which was 'out of bounds' to local people. Both the seafront, known as HMS Westcliff, and the pier, known as HMS Leigh, had been taken over by the Royal Navy. Sailors and workmen are clearing up after a bomb raid. Note the anti-invasion concrete block tank traps to prevent German tanks getting off the beach. Also, the pleasure boat mobile jetties have been moved off the beach to avoid use by German landing craft.

6. 1944. Landing in Normandy, delivering in Rochford.

Business carries on despite the war.

Even though he was called up for army service in August 1941 (and Jim was probably in the army by this time also), the Southend sweet business continued to be successful. Profits were £420 on a turnover of £2,508 for the year up to Jan 1942. How did the business continue without Stan (and possibly Jim) and despite the wartime rationing of food? The answer is almost certainly that Stan's father, Sam, and Doris ran the firm. However, the difficulties of getting supplies, particularly of sugar, did restrict the business. Sales were limited also by the lack of buyers. Many of the business's best customers, the children of the town, had been evacuated and there were no day trippers to buy boiled sweets and sticks of rock (if rock was being produced at this time). Non-residents were not allowed to travel to Southend as it was in a military exclusion zone. The only bright spot was the high number of military and naval personnel in the town. 1942 was the first business year Stan was absent for the whole period and, as a result, sales were down to £1,442. Henry Piper of Chelmsford Avenue prepared the accounts for the business and he commented in his letter of 15th March 1943 that 'the firm, in spite of the restrictions, has done quite well… the business is being most efficiently conducted without the slightest doubt, and is very good indeed'.

Why was the Normandy Invasion in June 1944 so important?

The First World War (1914–18) had ended in victory for the Allies – Britain, France and the US – over Germany. But it had left Germany as an unstable country, and its defeat had laid the foundations for the further conflict twenty years later. The Allies were not going to let that happen again. Prime Minister Churchill, in particular, wanted total victory this time; he wanted to ensure that Germany would become fully democratic and not threaten the free world again. How lucky we are today that we had a leader then whose foresight has resulted in a democratic and free Europe for the last seventy or so years. How lucky we are today that we had the soldiers and allies that fought, died and eradicated the Nazi evil. How lucky I am that my father, despite spending almost five years helping to defeat the Nazis, survived the war (although he lost his only brother) and was subsequently able to enjoy a happy and satisfying family and business life. We should all be thankful for our present peaceful, fair and democratic way of life. However, back in early 1944, total victory over Germany may well have seemed, to Stan, a distant prospect.

The Nazi war propaganda machine had created millions of fanatical Germans loyal to Hitler and willing to support him regardless of the consequences. The German people had been persuaded that they were the 'master race' and that their country would long be the dominant country of Europe. Churchill knew that the invasion of Germany and the overthrow of Hitler would be the only way to bring long-lasting peace to the continent. But progress in the war was slow. Sicily was invaded by the Allies in July 1943 and the British Eighth Army landed on the mainland of Italy on 3rd September. On 8th September the Italian Government surrendered to the Allies; however, on the same day the Germans instigated 'Operation Axis' to occupy Italy and to prevent Allied advances. The German Army defended with great determination, which delayed the northward progress of the Allies up the Italian peninsular. And even if the whole of Italy had been quickly occupied by the Allies in 1943, the mountains of the Alps would make it very difficult to then attack Germany.

On the eastern front, Russia was slowly making headway against stubborn opposition but at very heavy loss of life. The only way to bring about complete victory over Nazi Germany was for the allies to invade France and tackle the German Army head on. But a seaborne invasion of France from England would be a highly risky adventure. The Germans had a fleet of U-boat submarines ready to attack Allied shipping and had built strong defences along the French coast, called the Atlantic Wall, to deter an invasion from the sea. Should an invasion of France fail there was a danger of a military stalemate, resulting in a political settlement, which would have ended the war but would still have left the Nazis in power in Germany.

An invasion of Nazi-occupied Europe had to succeed.

In early 1944 Southend was still a dangerous place to live as these bomb-damaged buildings testify.

The Invasion of Europe, and Doris's fears for Stan.

By early June 1944 Doris had not seen Stan for five months. She must have wondered why he was away such a long time and why his planned leave in April had been cancelled. What was going on? She probably had some idea. She knew that there would be an attempt to invade Europe at some time. Although Stan was unable to give any hints in his letters as to what he was doing as they were all censored and never postmarked from where they came. Nevertheless, she could get an inkling from what she saw in Southend.

There was an increase in military movements in the town as the streets began to empty of soldiers as they were taken to departure ports. Sales of their sweets to soldiers and sailors in the town would have begun to drop. Although she was not allowed on Southend seafront, as it was a militarised area, she could see from where she lived – the top of Mount Avenue in Westcliff – what was happening in the River Thames below. There was now great activity as dozens of ships were moving out to sea. She did not know that they were full of soldiers ready to form up in the middle of the English Channel at a point nicknamed 'Piccadilly Circus', ready to sail towards the Normandy shore. In a few days' time she would see tugboats hauling enormous concrete contraptions that would form the Mulberry Harbours on the Normandy Coast. Little did she know that, in a few days' time, Stan would be driving more than a mile out to sea on these floating Mulberry Harbours to collect supplies from waiting ships. Still, she knew something big was about to happen. The news broadcast at lunchtime on 6th June confirmed it. British and Allied troops had started landing on the beaches of Normandy, France, at 7.30 am that morning. The long-awaited invasion of Europe had begun.

Did Doris feel elated at the news, with the hope that the war was taking a decisive turn for the better and would be over soon? She did not know, due to the strict secrecy about military matters, that Stan would soon be sent to France. However, he had not been sent to any of the other areas of fighting, such as Italy or the Far East, so she probably thought he would soon be part of the invasion force. Did she feel apprehensive that Stan would soon be in a war zone for the first time? She probably had all sorts of fears:

- *Would he get seasick?*
- *Will he have enough cigarettes to stop him worrying?*
- *What if I do not hear from him for weeks?*

- *Would his boat be attacked by German planes as it crossed the Channel?*
- *Will it be years before he sees the new baby?*
- *My first pregnancy was blighted by the shock death of my brother-in-law, would some terrible event happen again?*
- *Would he be injured or killed on the invasion beaches?*
- *How will I cope with two young children without a father?*

I suspect she was more fearful than elated, after all she was more than seven months pregnant with Michael, and the thought that she may be widowed with two young children must have gone through her mind. At least she had her in-laws living close by in Westcliff and her sister, Queenie, ready to come down from London to be with her for the birth. This time she could have the baby locally in Rochford Hospital, rather than being forced to travel to Surrey as she had to for her firstborn, due to Southend being an invasion risk area at the time.

The Invasion of Europe had been long in the planning. Every aspect was meticulously researched. The RAF photographed every inch of the possible landing sites. Britons were even asked to pass to the military any postcards they had of the French coast to build up a picture of the landscape the soldiers would encounter. A complex deception plan was set up to fool the Germans into thinking that an invasion landing would be in the Calais region, which was much closer to the English coast and far to the north of the intended landing area in Normandy. Hundreds of ships and landing craft were made ready to transport the thousands of soldiers across the English Channel.

By early June 1944 the south of England was one massive military camp, with over a million men from Britain, the USA and other Allied countries, together with their equipment, ready to take to their boats for the attack on occupied Europe. The Germans expected that an attempted invasion would take place and were well prepared. General Rommel had built huge concrete fortifications, including almost impregnable gun emplacements along the coast of France and beyond. The coasts were heavily mined, and the beaches littered with obstacles of every sort to make any landing difficult. Behind the beaches, the Germans had rapid mobile forces, including the latest tanks, in order to respond quickly and decisively to any landing.

Since June 1942 Stan's RASC company had been located with two tank brigades, initially the 31st and – since February 1943 – the 16th tank brigade. It seems his role was to be supporting tanks on the front line by providing motor maintenance, road laying or supporting the Royal Engineers to get tanks across damaged roads, rivers and other obstacles. After the long period of training with the tank brigades, it seems strange that he was taken off tank support and placed with Reserve Holding Unit 51 on 15th May 1944. This may well have pleased Stan as, had he stayed with the tanks, he would have undoubtedly been on the front-line face to face with the enemy at some time. This was because tipper lorries often drove into battle immediately behind advancing tanks in order to help them across obstacles. What would not have pleased him was having his nine days' leave cancelled in April, as he had not seen Doris since January. However, this was the same for all soldiers as it was a lock-down period. Security was tightened and there was a total blackout of any information that could hint of an invasion. Troop movements were restricted, training was intensified, and guns and equipment checked and polished again and again. It is not known where Stan was stationed at this time, but when he was moved nearer to one of the departure ports he knew invasion could not be far away.

D-Day and the start of freeing Europe.

Stan probably did not know that on 3rd June assault troops began loading onto the ships that would take them to France, or that the invasion that had been planned for 5th June was delayed to the following day due to bad weather. But he would soon learn of the massive scale of the invasion. On 5th June the largest amphibious invasion fleet in history set sail. It included 30 battleships and cruisers, 105 destroyers, 1,000 smaller naval ships, 4,000 landing craft and 800 merchant vessels, manned by 195,000 naval and merchant personnel. This fleet was to deliver 160,000 Allied soldiers on a fifty-mile stretch of the Normandy beaches on D-Day.

At fifty minutes past midnight on the 6th, British paratroops landed beside the River Orne to secure the bridge over it and liberated the first house in France, called the Cafe Gondree. Troops landed on five beaches (two American, Omaha and Utah; two British, Sword and Gold; and one Canadian, Juno) along a fifty-mile stretch of the Normandy coast. Although the Germans were caught completely by surprise, they put up strong resistance. The German defenders rained machine and heavy gunfire from secure concrete blockhouses onto the troops wading ashore, inflicting heavy casualties. Slowly, during the day, the defenders were overcome and pushed back from the beach area. By the end of the day, the Allies had landed over 150,000 soldiers and their equipment. They had penetrated several miles inland and established a significant bridgehead. However, the advance had been slower than expected and progress towards the capture of the towns of Caen and Bayeux was delayed by stout German resistance.

RASC Company 486, which Stan was soon to join in Normandy, had been stationed in various locations between Bury St Edmonds and Walton on the Naze on the days leading up to the invasion. Company 486 platoons embarked at Tilbury docks on 5th and 6th June. I discovered in the war records a report of 9th June 1944 that C Platoon 'Successfully landed at Jig beach. All vehicles successfully waded and occupied location MR875835'. (Note, these location references appeared in a number of war record reports, and I have been unable to find a key to them.)

Over the next few days, tens of thousands more troops were landed, together with a multitude of different vehicles and tanks and many hundreds of tons of supplies. The pieces of the floating harbours that Doris may have seen being towed down the River Thames below her Westcliff home were put together to form two Mulberry harbours off the Normandy beaches. These started to be used in their partly constructed state on 14th June.

D-Day plus Eight. Stan copes with artillery shelling, Doris with Doodlebugs.

The days following the invasion must have been a tense time for Stan. He was waiting somewhere in southern England with thousands of other soldiers ready to sail across the Channel to join the battle. He may have been thinking: *Were the Allies making headway? Were the Germans putting up strong resistance? How close to the shooting will I be when I land?*

He was kept busy, preparing for the landing: ensuring for the umpteenth time that his vehicle was ready; making sure all his equipment, most importantly his gun, was in proper working order; and writing his last letter to Doris before joining the battle to liberate Europe. He probably also wrote a farewell note that would be given to Doris should he be killed.

On 13th June, the Germans launched the first V-1 flying bomb against London. It landed in Bethnal Green, only a few miles north of where Doris's family lived in Dulwich, killing six people. The V-1s were fast, unmanned, jet-propelled flying bombs. They were the first of Hitler's 'vengeance weapons', designed to so terrorise the British people that Churchill would be forced to call an end to the war. They were launched from dozens of sites in France, Belgium and Holland and caused considerable alarm and damage in London and the South East. Stan said that he was always more worried about the dangers to Doris in Southend from enemy attacks than he was of his own personal safety in France. It is easy to understand why he felt this when he heard about the start of the German terror weapon campaign.

The day after the first V-1 attack was 14th June 1944 and, on that day, Stan sailed to France, probably from Portsmouth or Tilbury. He told me that he landed on the Love Beach section of Juno Beach, just east of Ver sur Mer (I wish I had asked him more about this!). He probably drove his (Ford three tonne?) lorry straight off a large landing craft on to the beach and on to an area behind the beach packed with soldiers, vehicles and military equipment. Driving across the beach was still hazardous. The war record for 21st June for RASC 486 Company, the company that Stan was to join, states 'Tipper destroyed by enemy mine on Love Beach'. In the eight days since the first landings the Allies had not moved very far inland. Caen was still in German hands, and they also held a line westward through Carpiquet, Fontenay and Tilly, only ten miles away from Stan. He was well within the range of the German heavy guns and could hear the battle raging in the distance. There was no warm bed in a cosy billet like before he sailed. Now he had to sleep on the ground, probably under his vehicle. He did say he became quite used to sleeping on the open ground and in ditches and found it quite comfortable.

The sections of the Mulberry harbour that had been towed along the Thames past Southend were now being put in place in the sea next to the town of Arromanches, in the centre of Gold Beach. The floating harbour provided a relatively calm anchorage for ships bringing troops and equipment to France. Floating roadways were built more than a mile out to sea so that large ships could dock in deep water and lorries could drive straight off them and on to the land. By late October, on the east quay at Arromanches, some 220,000 men and 39,000 vehicles had been landed. Stan said that the Mulberry floating harbour was a magnificent piece of engineering. Alain Ferrand in his *'Arromanches, History of a Harbour'* expresses his admiration thus 'The construction of the Mulberries was probably the greatest military engineering enterprise undertaken since the Persian armies crossed over the Bosphorus, on a pontoon bridge, in B.C. 480.'

Stan would have been very busy transporting supplies, men and equipment up to the front line, and repairing vehicles when they broke down. By 20th June there were half a million Allied troops ashore, crowded into a relatively small area, hoping to quickly break through the German lines. They were to be disappointed. Caen, a city the British had hoped to take on the first day, was still in German hands more than a month later, and they were putting up determined resistance to hold on to it. Meanwhile, the V-1 terror weapons were having an increasing impact on the soldiers' loved ones in England. Some 1,935 civilians had been killed and many more injured in the sixteen days since the start of the terror campaign. Stan and his fellow soldiers were desperate to push the Germans back from the coast and overrun the launching sites of the V-1s.

Doris's sister, Queenie, had to travel to work each day by bus from her home in Dulwich to central London. She was always most amused when telling me the story of her bus trips as she said the road into London followed the same route as the V-1s took and she would hear them going overhead, but that she knew she was safe when the bus eventually took a right turn. For her it was definitely 'keep calm and carry on', whilst seeing the funny side along the way. She also explained that, due to the blackout, London was completely dark in the evenings and that it was difficult to find your way around. But rather, as a single woman, being worried about her personal safety in the darkness, she always felt completely safe – such was the camaraderie and helpfulness of Londoners in this time of adversity.

The V-1, or Doodlebug as it became commonly known in England, was a terrifying weapon. Its pulse jet engine made a distinctive noise as it passed overhead and was dreaded by Londoners. Even more frightening was hearing the engine cut out, as this meant the rocket would then hurtle to earth causing its tonne of high explosive to explode. As they exploded on the surface, a huge blast wave rippled out from the epicentre. Its blast area extended across a radius of 400 to 600 yards in each direction and could demolish twenty houses. The height of the campaign was between June and October 1944, although there were attacks up to March 1945. A total of 9,521 V-1s were fired against South East England, killing 6,184 people and seriously injuring and maiming 17,981 others.

Five V-1s hit Southend, one each on Shoebury High Street, Kent Elms Corner and Thames Drive, and two near Bournes Green.

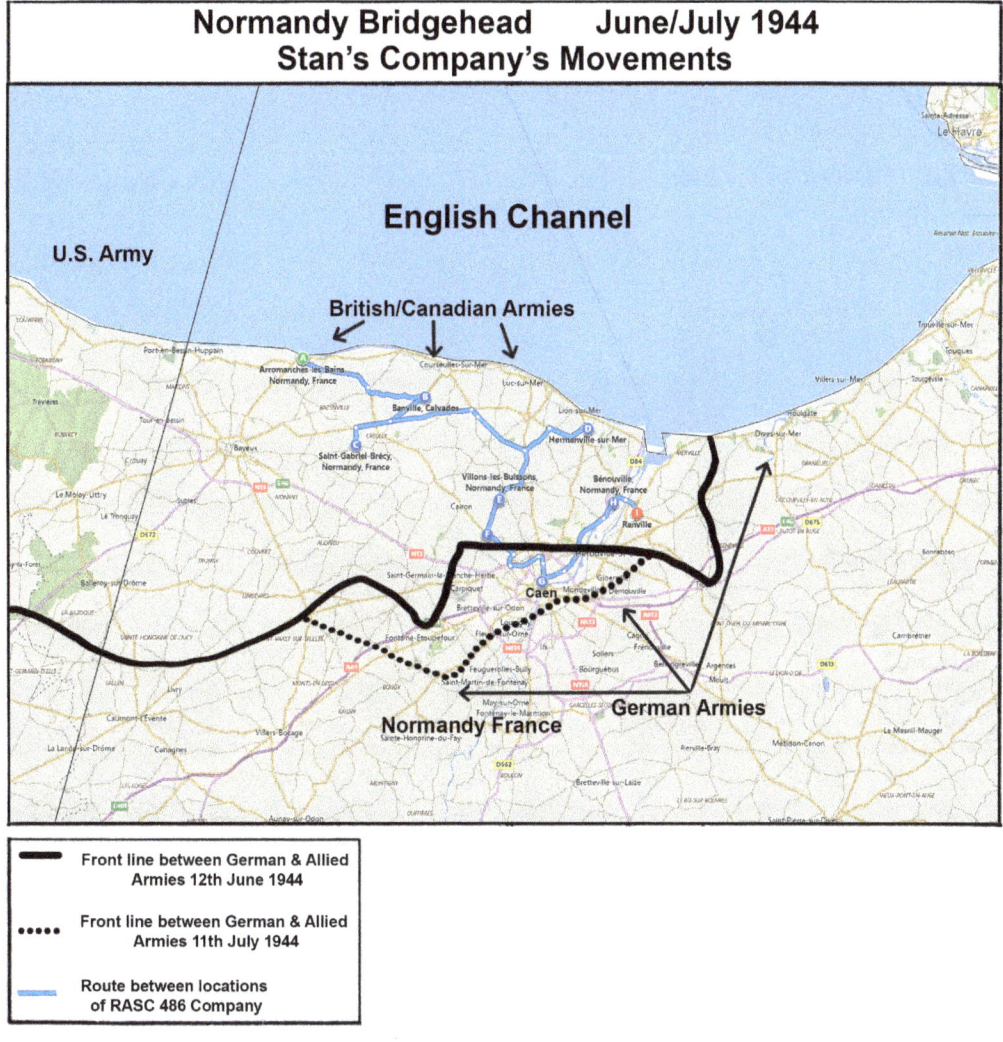

Normandy Bridgehead June/July 1944 – Stan's Company's Movements.

After the D-Day invasion of Normandy on 6th June 1944, hundreds of thousands of Allied troops were, for some weeks, hemmed in a narrow bridgehead within range of German artillery. Stan and his Royal Army Service Corps 486 Company were among them. They provided transport and repaired vehicles all over the bridgehead area.

The map shows some of the locations of the five platoons of 486 Company and the dates they were located there:

A – Arromanches-les-Bains site of the Mulberry harbour
B – Banville 21st June
C – Saint-Gabriel-Brecy 24th June

D – Hermanville-sur-Mer 11th July
E – Villons-les-Buissons 11th July
F – Buron 11th July
G – Caen 11th July
H – Benouville 16th July
I – Ranville 19th July

This V-1 flying bomb never made it to England. It is mounted on its original firing ramp and has wings like an aeroplane and a jet engine is mounted on its tail. I am at 'Le Blockhaus d'Eperlecques' near Calais in France in April 2018, which is a massive concrete building constructed to assemble and fire V-2 rockets. Fortunately, a tremendous RAF bombing raid, with heavy concrete piercing bombs, in August 1943 rendered the site unusable for firing them.

July 1944. Despite war raging in Normandy, the free world was planning to establish stable economic conditions for peacetime. This plaque in New Hampshire, USA commemorates the international meeting to set up the International Monetary Fund and the World Bank.

How I discovered what Stan did in the battles for Europe.

At this point in the story I will explain how I learned a little of what Stan did and where he went once he had landed on the Normandy beaches. Stan spoke very little of the war and, like most children, my brothers and I never bothered to ask. All I had to go on was a copy of his army pay-book.

In 2002 I did a two-week course on tracing family history at the Society of Genealogists in London. This led me to the National Archives in Kew where I was lucky to discover that my grandfather's First World War army record had survived the bombing in World War II that had destroyed many soldiers' records. When, in 2011, I wanted to find my father's army record, this proved more difficult. I needed a copy of my father's death certificate, as I would not be allowed to see the record of someone still living (he would have been a hundred years old in 2011). I also needed to prove that I was his closest relative. With all the required documentation, I wrote to the Army Personnel Centre in Glasgow in October 2011 requesting a copy of his army service record. There was a delay due to the 'high volume of urgent welfare requests of former (living) soldiers'. It was some eleven months later that a letter landed on my doormat containing a copy of the dozen pages of his 'Service and Casualty' record.

The record was helpful in that it detailed his training and movements while in England. However, it did not show his movements once he was overseas. In order to progress, I needed to establish which RASC company he was attached to. A visit to the National Army Museum in Chelsea did not prove helpful, except that I did find out there was a museum dedicated to the RASC in Camberley, Surrey. One day, while visiting my daughter and grandchildren in Guildford, I drove over to the museum to meet the curator. Even though I had not booked an appointment, he spent most of the afternoon showing me documents and trying to work out which of the 900 or so companies Stan was attached to. Eventually, he was 90% sure it was 486 Company. (It was not until a couple of years later that I re-read the only letter I had that Stan had written to Doris. I had previously not noticed the address at the top of the first page which said 'W/S 486' which confirmed that Stan had indeed been in the workshop platoon of 486 Company.)

The curator then went to find a book called *The Story of the RASC 1939–1945*. Once he had found it, he said, 'You are very lucky; the book only has accounts of about a dozen units out of the 900, and one of them happens to be about 486 Company'. He then very helpfully downloaded a digital copy of the whole 700-page book onto a CD for me to take away. The book describes 486 as a 'tipper' company. It then explains how the Royal Engineers and the tippers were often working at the front line ahead of the infantry and armour as 'roads had to be repaired, even remade, bridges had to be built, before the attack could go in.' 486 Company consisted of some 400 soldiers split into four platoons, plus headquarters and workshops. It is not entirely clear what Stan's precise role was in the army. His 'Army Service and Pay Record' includes a testimonial which states his army duties were: '1. Driver, including vehicles. 2. Fitter, motor vehicles. 3. Vehicle mechanic.' This document also lists many of the mechanic courses he went on in the army. His letter home says he was in the workshop platoon of 484 Company. From this evidence, I suspect he was mainly a mechanic/mechanic supervisor in the workshop with occasional driving duties when time allowed.

The curator had told me about the war records held at the National Archives at Kew, so that was where I visited a few weeks later. It always amazes me how good we are in this country at writing up official records and then keeping them for hundreds of years, such as the eleventh century Doomsday Book. The army records were no exception. Each army company, probably a few hundred men, had to keep a diary of their daily activities and send a copy to the War Office in London every day. The staff at the National Archives found the war diary for RASC 486 Company for me within an hour. Even though it was marked 'Secret until 2045', I was able to read and photograph it.

Of most interest to me was that the diary showed, for each of the platoons of the company, the locations where they were based and the dates they moved. I was now able to compare Stan's movement across the continent with the progress of the British Army battling its way towards Germany. I was beginning to learn the type of work Stan and his colleagues were doing, how close they were to the front line, and some of the actions they were involved in.

Battle for Caen, vehicles decked with roses.

Royal Army Service Corps Company 486 had been busy, amongst other things, repairing damaged roads. This was essential to ease the movement towards the enemy of the massive Allied army that had congregated on the shores of Normandy. There had been minor incidents. One of 486 Company's Dennis tippers was destroyed by an enemy mine at the exit from Love Beach and three vehicles were damaged by enemy mortar fire in the village of Omeux. Four days after this latter incident, on 2nd July, Stan was posted to 486 Company with whom he was to stay for many months.

The British were preparing for an all-out attack on Caen. On 7th July bombers dropped 2,500 tons of bombs on Caen and, on the following day, the British battleship Rodney fired its massive shells into the city over the heads of British troops. The next day the German General in command ordered his troops to pull back into the suburbs of Caen. This allowed some advanced British troops to penetrate the northern outskirts of the city. The daily war diary of 486 Company rarely gives a glimpse of precisely what its troops were doing. However, for once, the war diary for 11th July goes into some detail, as the following extract shows.

11th July 1944, 486 Company war diary extract

1900. Reported to 53 Coy Pioneer Corps located in Hermanville and loaded 160 personnel and kits. Moved forward at 1930 routes via Cazelle, Villons les Buissons and Buron.

2100. Arrived in Place St Martin, Caen and reported to commander, 3 Canadian Dist, who ordered the dispersal of troops and vehicles under trees in the Place. Our arrival brought out a large number of civilians, many of whom pressed bottles of wine on the troops and decked the vehicles with roses. Caen was being shelled intermittently and appeared unoccupied by troops…

12th July

1000. Informed that (we) were the first of the special clearance… troops in Caen and the job would last 7–10 days before military occupation was started. That many persons were believed still alive under the debris, hence the urgency of the call.

1100. Started moving troops in vehicles blocks of 6, at least 100yds apart, into Caen, which was under shellfire…

1315. Four tippers detailed for work in Place St Martin.

1355. Shellfire intensified, German planes over Caen. Heavy AA barrage. Low flying aircraft gunned vicinity of location.

1405. Another machine gun attack. Sgt Doris wounded in chest by bullet…

1500. …OC arrived amidst further shellfire.

1800. After lull, shellfire resumed. Small scale enemy attacks in vicinity…

2030. Very heavy shellfire. Direct hit on No 1 garage, containing some of our stores, rations… Two shells on location but not on buildings. No damage to Vehs and only very minor casualties dealt with by detachment first aid personnel. Received report that Sgt Doris had died of wounds.

2115. …Ordered (to) evacuate location. Lt Rutherford left location at 2210, having seen all vehicles dispatched at two minute intervals, owing to continued heavy shelling.

2300. Reoccupied location at Lion-sur-Mer.

13th July

Vehs continue to work in Caen reporting daily at 0815 and returning in the evenings.

Whether Stan was involved in this incident, we do not know. However, it does paint a vivid picture of the activities in Caen at that time and the ever-present dangers.

The Story of the RASC describes another incident on 18th July. B Platoon of 486 Company were notified to take up a location at Benouville, working with REs (Royal Engineers). 'As soon as the RAF had completed a bombing raid, the RE and the tippers went in to bridge the Caen Canal and the River Orne. These RE and tippers were at that time ahead of the infantry and armour. This was a typical situation: roads had to be repaired, even remade, bridges had to be built, before attacks could go in. It was a hard and tough experience for unseasoned troops like the drivers of the company.'

The 486 Company war diary entry of 20th July states 'Working forward in battle area around Caen and experiencing a lot of shelling and at times mortar fire'. Mortars are used in close combat fighting so Stan is likely to have been within a few hundred yards of the enemy at times.

As the battle swung southwards towards Tilly and Villers Bocage, '*The Story of the RASC*' explains that one vehicle of D Platoon was working with the RE in advance of the infantry: 'The sappers and tipper were ambushed by a German patrol, and in a matter of moments the vehicle was under fire and abandoned... There was hardly a tipper vehicle in the company that did not have some battle scars.' (Sappers are soldiers of the rank of private in the Royal Engineers.)

The invasion plan had set the capture of Caen as an objective by the end of D-Day. However, the Germans put up fierce resistance. There were a number of major battles, each falling short of its objectives. Operation Epsom (26th to 30th June) was an attack several miles west of the city and, while it did achieve a small bridgehead over the River Odon, it failed to capture the important high ground at Hill 112. Operation Windsor (4th and 5th July) captured the village of Carpiquet but failed to capture the airfield that would have been very important to the RAF. Operation Charnwood (8th and 9th July) succeeded in taking the northern part of the city but failed to capture the bridges over the River Orne. Operation Jupiter, 10th July, initially captured Hill 112, only to be relinquished to the Germans. Operation Goodwood (18th to 20th July) was an attack east of Caen with the aim of advancing south to the Caen-Falaise road. While good progress was made, the advance was halted short of the Caen-Falaise road. Success was at last achieved on the 19th July as Caen was finally encircled and completely in Allied hands after thirty-six days of heavy fighting.

Stan had told me with a feeling of despair in his voice and sadness in his face that Caen was completely 'smashed up'. He clearly felt very sorry for its French inhabitants.

News of the Doodlebug campaign against London and the South East, and the impact it was having, must have inspired the troops to push the enemy back despite the fierce German resistance in and around Caen. In the five weeks since the V-1 terror campaign started, some half a million civilians had been evacuated from London to towns and cities in less vulnerable places.

Promotion comes quickly during battles. Stan gets his full promotion to Corporal on 30th June 1944, hence the two stripes on his arm.

The 'Sweet Kings' of Southend.

On November 12th 2011, my wife, Mary, and I were in Grimsby, a small town on the shore of Lake Ontario. We were in Canada to celebrate the hundredth birthday of my Aunt Mabel (my maternal grandmother's sister's daughter). The birthday party was being held in the old town library, which was now used as a community hall. As we walked through the door into the gathering, a tall man, probably in his seventies, whom I had never met, walked up to me and said:

'You must be one of the Sweet Kings of Southend.'

He then introduced himself as Alan Forster, a second cousin.

'I've never been called that before,' I responded.

He went on:

'Yes, during the last war, when I was a young boy, your father every now and then sent me a box of sweets he had made. They were a real treat as sweets were in such short supply. I used to call your parents the "Sweet Kings of Southend".'

I was moved by Alan's expression of gratitude, some sixty years later, for my parents' acts of kindness.

Some months after meeting Alan Forster, I was going through my mother's belongings when I came across a letter from a Mrs D Norley of Canterbury, dated 27th January 1942 (I have no idea who this lady was). In the letter she thanked Doris for the gift of sweets she had sent. It is pleasing to me to know that my parents were generous in providing gifts of rationed sweets. They probably sent sweets to family members in London and Cambridgeshire as well.

***

While Stan was taking part in the momentous events in Normandy, his father (Sam) and Doris were keeping the business running in Southend. In the year up to February 1944, profits increased to £245. It is interesting to note that the accounts show a charge of £5 and 4 shillings for 'fire watching'. Was someone being paid to raise the alarm should the factory be hit by a bomb? Or was this just a contribution towards Southend's firewatchers? It does emphasise, though, the bombing risk there was to Southend throughout the war; after all, as Doris observed, it was on the route the German bombers took to London. There was further expansion in the business during 1944, which saw annual profits rise to £319. That was thanks to Sam King's efforts who, at the age of sixty-four, was having, I expect, to do the heavy work of boiling the ingredients, while Doris most likely involved herself with bottling and labelling and doing the bookwork.

Stan could not have helped much as he had nine days leave the whole year and Doris may have had to reduce her input into the business due to her pregnancy.

I can well imagine the sense of satisfaction that Sam and Doris had in knowing they were keeping the business alive for Stan's return after the war, and the pleasure it gave to Stan knowing that his business dream was in good hands.

The business would never have survived had Sam been killed in the Great War rather than just being injured.

No Stan, another family event, plenty of danger.

The week of 22nd July 1944 saw momentous things: the capture of Caen; the British advance south east of the city in Operation Goodwood; the American advance into Brittany; and an important family event in Southend. That week marked the beginning of the end for the Germans in France. Stan was in the thick of it, probably driving his truck close to the front line and within range of enemy artillery, either transporting troops and supplies or collecting broken down vehicles for repair. But his thoughts must have been back in England. Doris was now thirty-nine weeks pregnant, the Germans were launching Doodlebugs (V-1s) and V-2 rockets towards his hometown and he was not there supporting his wife when she needed him.

There was some good news in that the RAF fighter planes and ground defences were shooting down increasing numbers of V-1 flying bombs. However, there was no defence against the V-2s. These were the world's first long-range guided ballistic missiles (according to Wikipedia). They used a liquid propellant rocket engine, could carry a 1,000kg warhead and could easily reach London from German-occupied Europe. There was no defence against the V-2 rockets as they travelled too fast for the Spitfires in the air or the anti-aircraft batteries on the ground to shoot them down. There was no time to take shelter from a rocket attack. The first people knew of them was when they exploded on the ground. It was truly a 'terror weapon'.

Despite the risk of rocket attacks and the absence of Stan, there was one consolation for Doris. She could have her second baby nearer home. Now that the threat of a German invasion had passed, maternity facilities were again being provided a few miles away at Rochford Hospital.

Having a baby in wartime had considerable risks in addition to those usually associated with childbirth. For example, Joan Rhodes was awaiting the birth of her first child in the Middlesex Hospital in September 1944. She recalls, 'During air raids we were told NOT to get out of our beds, but to pull our meal trolleys over our heads, then get under the bedclothes. A flying bomb (buzz bomb) dropped in the hospital grounds and blew all the windows in! None of us were hurt. One lady had hysterics, but only three went into labour, which surprised the doctors.'

As with Doris's first delivery, her sister (Queenie) most likely came down from London to be with her, and her in-laws (Sam and Grace) were also on hand. Doris had her second child on Saturday 22nd July 1944.

Doris had her first child in hospital in Surrey. She was perhaps fortunate that she did not have her second son in Surrey also. As the BBC *People's War* website recounts a story by Shirley Croucher. On the same day as Doris's second son was born, Shirley says, 'My mother, Irene Croucher, gave birth to her third child. When she went into labour the ambulance could not find a hospital that could take her as the Doodlebugs were coming thick and fast and everywhere was being bombed. She said it was so frightening. She ended up giving birth to a son in the driveway of a hospital in Dorking… when she was travelling home from the hospital by bus, a Doodlebug came right across the road in front of the bus, just missing them and landing some way away in a field.'

Doris may not have spent the customary twelve days in hospital, as the following photograph shows her (probably in a photographic studio) with her baby at ten days old. Doris and Stan named him Michael Peter King. They had most likely chosen the name some time before as they knew they would be apart for the birth. The real concern for Doris was for Stan's safety. He had been in the warzone for five weeks and she worried that he was in much more danger than he explained in his letters home.

Stan had not seen Doris since his last leave in January, six months earlier, so regular letters between them, probably on a daily basis, were their only means of contact, comfort and love. Stan heard the news of Michael's birth through a message conveyed through 114 Company (according to his war record), with whom he was probably then assisting. Stan's company was based in Benouville on the River Orne at this time. Despite the dangerous conditions, I expect Stan was able to 'wet the baby's head' with his colleagues. Little did he know that he would not see his new son for another ten months, by which time the war would be over. How delighted and proud he must have been when Doris sent him a photograph of his new son at ten days old.

Stan must have been thrilled by his first sight of his second son, Michael, who is ten days old in this 1st August 1944 picture. He was not going to be able to hold him for another ten months.

Breakout across northern France.

In northern France, most of the German armed forces were confronting the British around Caen. The American forces took the opportunity to launch Operation Cobra on 25th July with the aim of breaking out through the less heavily defended area west of the Normandy bridgehead. By 5th August they had reached Nantes near the mouth of the River Loire, which had the effect of isolating German-held Brittany from the rest of France. The General Von Kluge was so alarmed that he sent five divisions to try to halt the Americans. This proved unsuccessful but provided some relief for the British and Canadians who were now fighting their way south of Caen through difficult 'hedgerow' (bocage) country. The Americans now swung south and west through relatively lightly held territory. The British were fighting down from the north and the Americans up from the south and, by 19th August, the Germans were surrounded in what became known as the 'Falaise Pocket'.

Many German soldiers were killed and some 50,000 surrendered. The Battle for Normandy had been won.

Doris's mother, Harriet Cockshull, travelled from Dulwich in August 1944 so she could meet her second grandson.

Across France and into Belgium.

Once the Germans had been routed in the Falaise Pocket, the breakout from the Normandy bridgehead could begin. Six days later, on 25th August, General Montgomery's army had reached the River Seine. The *'RASC Story'* helpfully explains, 'all platoons [were] taking part in assisting the Royal Engineers in their magnificent work of bridging the Seine'. On the same day, Paris was liberated by the Americans. By 1st September XXX Corps liberated Arras. Progress was now very swift against a rapidly retreating German Army. British troops crossed into Belgium on 2nd September, entered Brussels on 3rd September and liberated Antwerp on 4th September. XXX Corps, under Lieutenant-General Brian Horrocks, had advanced 200 miles almost unopposed in fourteen days.

Stan's company was not far behind. On 5th September his workshop platoon was in Buicourt, north of Paris. Platoon B, in the lead for 486 Company, was some sixty-one miles ahead of Stan and was approaching Arras (liberated four days before). By 7th September Platoon B was in Tournai in Belgium and a week later in Steenlaid, north of Brussels. On 6th September Stan's workshop platoon reached Froidment (north of Laon, France). By 18th September Stan was nineteen miles south east of Brussels at Bierghes. Two days later, and a further seventy-eight miles, he was in Oostham (north west of Hasselt, Belgium). This was a period of slow driving, along roads often damaged by mines and shells, and having to take detours to avoid obstacles such as broken bridges, always with the danger of coming across unexploded mines. I expect there were frequent stops to repair broken down company vehicles.

Moving into Holland.

By mid-September 1944, Stan was in northern Belgium. He was most likely helping with the build up to Operation Market Garden, which was subsequently immortalised in the film *A Bridge Too Far*. General Montgomery's plan was to attack northwards through Holland rather than attack directly westward towards Germany. This would enable his army to skirt around the top of the German prepared defences, called the Siegfried Line, to reach the north German plain, which would open the way to Berlin. If all went to plan, it would be possible to reach Berlin by Christmas, thus ending the war in 1944. To achieve this, airborne troops would be dropped by parachute to secure the bridges crossing the rivers and canals while the main body of the XXX Army would fight along the road towards the Rhine Bridge at Arnhem.

Stan would have been very busy repairing vehicles and transporting men and equipment up to the starting point south of Eindhoven for the battle. *The Story of the RASC* states that 'B Platoon moved up from Son to Veghel, farther north up the corridor between Eindhoven and Nijmegen – a mile from the actual line. Enemy patrols passed through the location, but, discretion being the better part of valour, these patrols were left entirely alone.' This is evidence of how close the tipper platoons worked with the front line.

On 17th September, some 10,000 troops were parachuted into Arnhem, but problems started almost immediately. The troops were dropped too far away from the Rhine bridge and the Germans had much stronger forces in the vicinity than the British had expected. The troops fighting along the 100-km road towards Arnhem also encountered stronger opposition than had been predicted so were unable to reach the British troops holding out in Arnhem. The lightly equipped airborne soldiers fought heroically but could not resist the heavily armoured tanks of the Germans. So, after ten days of vicious fighting and without being relieved by the XXX Army, who were still some miles away, 6,000 British soldiers surrendered to the Germans. It was a bitter defeat for the British and ended any hope of an early finish to the war.

Eindhoven was liberated on 18th September as part of the Market Garden operation. The following day Stan arrived at Oostham, thirty-four miles to the south. On 27th September Platoon C was in Grave in Holland, some three miles from Nijmegen and close to the front line.

Stan spent several months in and around Eindhoven, including Christmas 1944, and would have seen for himself the devastation in the streets. British and American troops liberated the city on 18th September 1944. On the following day, the Germans bombed Eindhoven. This photograph of Catharinaplein shows soldiers talking to local people in the aftermath of that raid. To the left of the picture is St Catherine's Church, which is still a landmark in the city.

Jacob van Slooten took this photograph on 18th September 1944, the day his city of Eindhoven was liberated. His son, Rene van Slooten, describes the picture as follows:

'This is my mother with my brother Erik (born 1942). My mother was expecting me for seven months at the time. I was born on 20th November, and she often told me she could hear the guns during the Battle of the Bulge when she had to get up at night to feed me. In the back you see an American and a British soldier having a relaxed conversation, leaning against a scout car. My parents had a Jewish friend hidden in their house, but they were betrayed. Fortunately, they were tipped by a 'good' cop that the Gestapo were going to arrest the friend and my parents. They could get this friend out in time through the Resistance, but my parents faced a sure arrest and probably a deportation to a concentration camp. Then Eindhoven was liberated prematurely due to Operation Market Garden. That operation failed, but it surely saved the lives of my parents, my brother and me! Now you know why my mother looks so happy in the picture.'

I like to think that this family, who were so lucky to avoid the concentration camps, could have been the ones Stan was billeted with for Christmas 1944.

Stan in battle but thinking about Doris.

So far I've told the story of Stan's and Doris's war from the brief things I remember them telling me and from research I have done. Luckily, one letter has survived that tells in Stan's own words what his experiences and thoughts were at the time. Letters from home were one of the most important things that boosted the morale of soldiers. In the absence of telephones and before the era of the internet and texts, letters were the only form of communication and comfort between soldiers and their loved ones. The army understood this and made every effort to get post to soldiers quickly. As a result, there was a constant stream of letters, with many couples writing on a daily basis to each other. Letters from soldiers were usually read by censors before they were sent home and any information that could be useful to the enemy, such as the location of the army unit, was deleted. I remember a story that my grandfather, Samuel, told me about the letters he sent home from the battlefields of the First World War. He said, 'I used to hide clues, so that they would not be noticed by the censor, in my letters to indicate where I was.' With a smile on his face he added, 'but your grandmother could never work out my clues.'

Why did Doris decide to keep this particular letter? And why after her death did Stan keep it in his safe deposit box at the Midland Bank? Probably at the end of the war they wanted to put the stressful wartime years behind them and destroyed all the other letters. Maybe this special letter brought back happy memories for both of them. Or possibly they wanted their sons to read it to better understand their parents' marriage.

So the letter that Stan wrote to Doris on Saturday 23rd September 1944 is particularly important as a window into their lives at the time. When Stan wrote this the army was desperately trying to relieve the thousands of airborne troops encircled by the Germans in Arnhem a few dozen miles to the north. Both censorship and the need to keep up morale at home prevented Stan from mentioning anything about the military situation. Three days later, the Allied troops surrendered at Arnhem.

I am grateful that they kept this letter as it expresses Stan and Doris's great love for each other and shows Stan's thoughtfulness and sensitivity.
Stan writes:

Cpl. King S. (T/281163)
W/S Platoon
486 Coy RASC
(Tipper)
B L A

My Darling Wife

Many thanks for your parcel received today appropriately for it is my 33rd birthday. I have got a few more years left yet, sweetheart before 'gone'. In fact life's only just started really and I can't live it till I return home after the war. Thanks for all the little bits in the parcel, dear. The cakes and biscuits are a real treat although our army food at the moment is good (in fact we've been getting some German rations they took). Yes I'm nicely stocked again. At the moment we can't 'lait' (milk) so I will keep my sugar and tea for a while. It's funny it's all or none over here. Some places we were able to get plenty of milk and here we can't any. Sometimes it's eggs but here none. Plenty of tomatoes and fruit though. Our choc, sweets and fags are coming thro' the haufe (?) ration O.K. and we can usually get to the shops once a week say for knick knacks. But we never know over here and it pays to keep a good stock in. How are you getting along, dear, with your babies? A busy time for you but a happy one. I k??s (?) in spite of everything. Of course I'm simply praying to be home now to help you although of course I'll be more 'useful' later on I suppose! It must be rather a job arranging for Michael's christening. Is it necessary for 2 Godfathers and the like? I have always imagined it is rather awkward when the child is getting too old. Y'know he might answer the vicar back or something! And John might want to push the font over p'haps! We've got a couple of tough lads now I'll be bound!

I wonder what the real reason is why we have such two fine sons. Of course, the answer 'Well why shouldn't we?' doesn't seem to be enough somehow, does it? The most logical answer I can think of is… our great love for each other— the depths of which we can only realise when something (usually something small and silly) goes wrong, and your desire and ambition for Motherhood coupled with your delightful femininity. This last virtue has played a 'big' part in our married life, sweetheart. And maybe, you might have thought I have been blind to this in your character. It's just because I haven't spoken about it (being an Englishman and rather stupid!). But it makes for married bliss, darling. There are many ways in which you are delightfully feminine. Your likes and dislikes demonstrate this a lot to me, but there's your little ways—the way you do things. The way you used to hold John when he was a baby—being particular about dressing yourself and him. And then being a shade towards having an 'Inferiority Complex' regarding neighbours and your dislike for me watching you dress your hair. All ordinary everyday things—very diverse and very feminine. But the other side of your femininity delights me more because as your husband it makes for pleasure and happiness in our intimacy…

The next three pages of the letter are a sensitive and passionate expression of Stan's love for Doris and end with the following:

So look to the future, dearest wife of mine, and smile away the time with our two fine sons for it will not be very long now till my home-coming. I send you my love and my love to John and Michael.

From Stan xxxxxxxxxx/xxx

Starvation in Holland, V-2 rockets in Southend.

While in Oostham, Stan may have seen another of Hitler's vengeance weapons, the world's first jet fighter, as the first one seen by the Allies was shot down over the town of Nijmegen on 6th October. On 10th October the workshop platoon moved to Eindhoven, where it was to be based until the middle of March 1945. Meanwhile, in Southend on 11th October, the first of several V-2 rockets to land on the town exploded on the foreshore. I wonder if Doris heard the explosion… Three days later, Stan's company was visited by the medical officer and padre and a church service was held. Perhaps more importantly to the men, five 'other ranks' were sent on forty-eight hours' rest leave to Brussels. How Stan would have liked to have been one of them.

The euphoria of chasing the fleeing Germans across France, Belgium and into Holland was rapidly replaced by the reality of the failure of Market Garden and the German determination to tenaciously defend their borders. November came, the weather worsened and the folks back home were suffering from the continuing V-2 rocket attacks. For example, on 25th November, 160 shoppers were killed when a Woolworths store in New Cross Road, Deptford was hit. December brought snow and more setbacks. On 16th December Hitler unleashed an offensive into the American sector of the front line through the hilly and forested area of the Ardennes in Belgium. The Allies were caught completely by surprise and 80,000 Americans were overwhelmed by the quarter of a million German attackers. The Germans advanced some sixty miles, aiming to cut off the British in the north from the Americans in the south. British troops were moved southward to hold a line of defence to assist the Americans and stop the Germans advancing northwards. Stan said he was involved in this action in what became known as the 'Battle of the Bulge'. The Americans counter attacked and by mid-January the Germans' last offensive action of the war had been defeated.

Stan with fellow soldiers pictured on 25th September 1944 at Oostham, Belgium. On the same day, seventy miles to the north, British troops faced defeat at Arnhem in the Bridge Too Far battle. Corporal Stan King (bottom row, third from the right) with the workshop platoon of 486 Company Royal Army Service Corps (Tipper), BLA (British Land Army). Oostham is twelve miles from the Dutch border and twenty-six miles south of Eindhoven, Holland. Note the soldier on the extreme right is wearing a leather sleeveless coat. I remember Dad wearing one of these every winter when working in the garden.

On 23rd December, Stan's army company, 486 Royal Army Service Corps, held a ballot for privilege leave to the UK for Christmas. Surely Stan would have qualified on compassionate grounds. He had not seen Doris since January, had been unable to support her during pregnancy and childbirth and had not met his second son, Michael, who was now five months old. Sadly, luck was not on his side and he stayed in Holland.

Stan said that what really upset him was seeing underfed and skinny Dutch children. The winter of 1944/45 is known as the 'hunger winter' in Holland. The Germans had cut off supplies of food in retaliation for the Dutch refusing to help the Nazi war effort with the result that the Dutch were living on starvation level diets. Some 22,000 Dutch people died of malnutrition that winter. Whilst the situation was improving in those areas liberated by the Allies, food was still scarce.

Finding an appropriate Christmas present in wartime was difficult as almost everything was in short supply. And what do you give to a soldier on active duty? Doris decided to use some of her precious ration coupons on ingredients to make a small Christmas pudding to send to Stan. The war diary for 24th December states that the workshop platoon was put into private billets (billets were civilian houses where soldiers were lodged temporarily). So, hopefully Stan had a comfortable bed to sleep in for Christmas.

Back in Southend, tragedy struck on that Christmas Eve when a V-2 rocket exploded next to Eastwood High School in Park Avenue killing the head teacher, Mr Richard Bussell, aged 53. Some 200 properties were damaged. According to a post on the *mailonline* website, the old school railings on the west side of the school still show the shrapnel marks as evidence of that fateful day.

Peter White, a platoon commander with the King's Own Scottish Borderers, was also billeted with a Dutch family over Christmas 1944. In his book *With the Jocks* he describes the hardships the Dutch family suffered: 'Holland seems to have been hit by far the hardest in occupation. The shops were almost empty of all but a few goods of very shoddy quality. The mother must have had a terrible time trying to feed her large family. At times tulip bulbs had been eaten in place of potatoes while crushed turnips and other seeds had been used to provide cooking fat. Meat was almost unknown.'

Stan told me that, on that Christmas morning 1944, he decided to give Doris's present to the lady of the house he was billeted with. When Stan sat down to Christmas dinner with his hosts and their children, he found them to be so excited to have Doris's Christmas pudding as the highlight of their meal, the like of which they had not tasted for several years. It was carefully cut into small pieces so that everyone would have a taste.

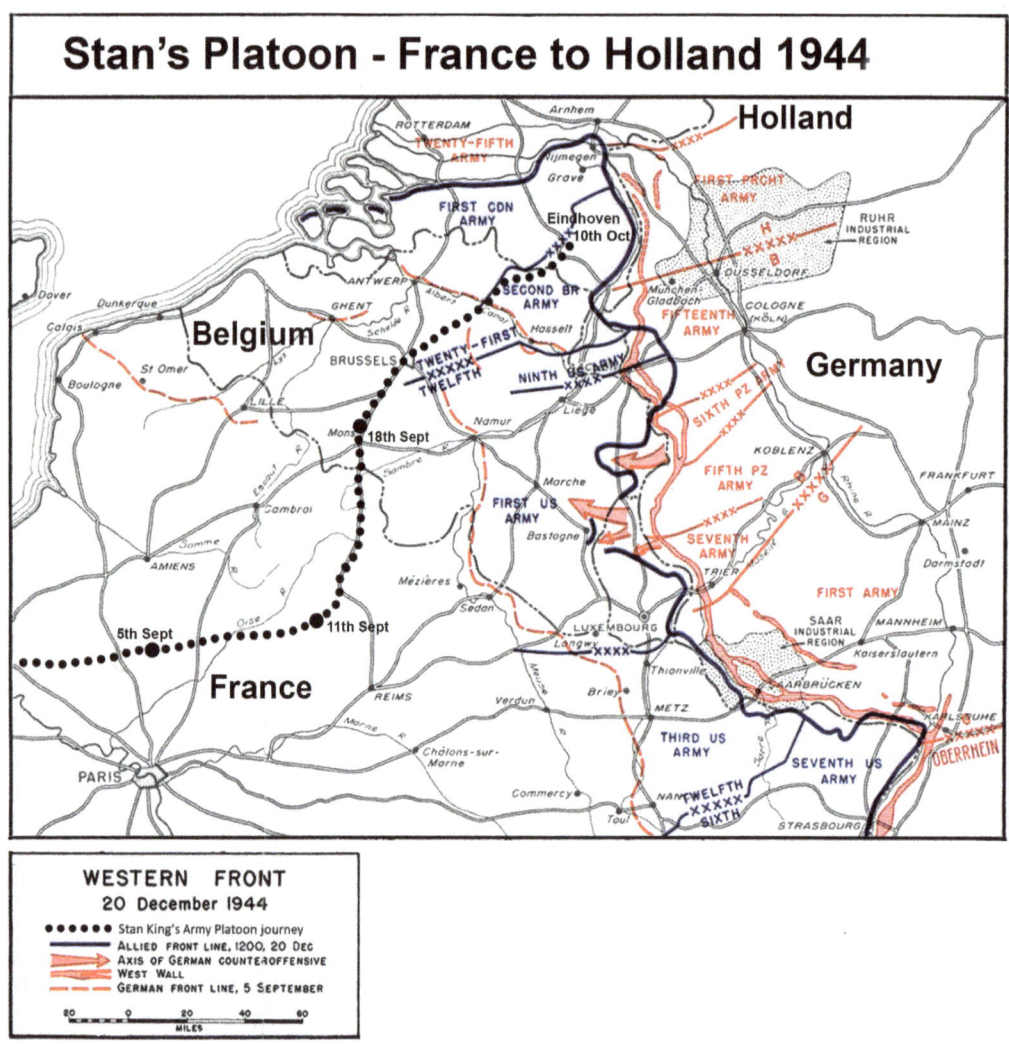

Map shows:

Dad's journey following the army advance towards Germany – Sept/Oct 1944.

During September 1944, the British, Canadian and United States armies were chasing the retreating German armies across France, Belgium and into Holland. According to the daily war reports from RASC 486 Company, Dad's workshop platoon was not far behind the front line.

The dotted line on the map shows the route taken and the locations of the workshop platoon:

5th September 1944 at Buicourt, north of Paris.

11th September at Froidment, north of Laon, France.
18th September at Bierghes, nineteen miles south of Brussels.
10th October at Eindhoven, Holland.

The thick black line on the map shows the front line between the Allied and German armies at 20th December 1944. Little ground had been gained since October as the Germans were stoutly defending their border using the River Rhine and the defensive fortification line called the Western Wall.

The thick red line is the West Wall (Siegfried Line).

The broken red line indicates the German front line on 5th September 1944.

7. 1945. War ends, separation doesn't.

After a cold, depressing winter, Stan moves into Germany.

After the race across France and Belgium almost to the border of Germany in September, hopes had been high for an early end to the war. Since then things had not gone well. The Germans were stoutly defending their borders behind a heavily militarised Siegfried Line (West Wall) and the natural barrier of the River Rhine. The hoped for advance into Germany across the bridge at Arnhem had failed and the Germans had spectacularly counter-attacked through the Ardennes in the Battle of the Bulge. And the weather was awful – cold, muddy and snowy (the company war diary of 8th January mentions snow). Stan could not get any leave back home to see his new son and he was having to leave the running of his business to his wife and aged father for a fourth year. Stan was coming across half-starved children in Holland, and V-2 rockets were dropping on London, the south east and Southend. This would have been a worrying time for Stan.

After the long, freezing winter, the thaw came. And 'roads began to collapse, and the tippers were operating night and day; a most unfortunate time for the company, as we were due a visit by MT (Motor Transport) Inspectorate. But everyone worked hard and conscientiously, and the company earned a good technical report'. So, even in the midst of the war, bureaucratic inspections have to take place, as *The Story of the RASC* explains.

February 1945 saw the western Allied armies pushing the Germans back to the River Rhine, the great defensive barrier that was stopping the Allies penetrating into the heart of Germany. The British captured

Kevelaer (twelve miles from the Rhine) on 4th March and by 19th March Stan's company had set up their repair workshop there. Stan was now in Germany and he could see the contrast, as he once told me, that so upset him – between the chubby well-fed German children and the skinny Dutch children that he had left behind. He was in enemy territory and the local people would not be welcoming British soldiers and there was always a possibility of an attack by Nazi soldiers who had not yet surrendered.

There was now a steady build-up of all sorts of materials – amphibious vehicles, artillery pieces, gliders, etc. – in preparation for a crossing of the Rhine. Stan's company seems to have been heavily involved with moving pieces of Bailey (temporary) bridges towards the front line ready for the Rhine crossing. (The war diary for 1st April states that 'all platoons took part in bridging operations over the Rhine.) At last, after weeks of preparation, a great artillery barrage began across the Rhine on the night of 23rd/24th March. Troops then took to boats to cross the river near the town of Rees. Similar crossings took place near Xanten and Wesel. By the morning of 24th March it was clear that the British were well established on the far side of the Rhine.

Later that morning, the last great airborne attack of the European war took place when over 3,900 aircraft dropped some 21,000 paratroopers across the Rhine near Xanten. Stan would have seen the air armada fly overhead. From a little hill near Xanten, Prime Minister Winston Churchill watched the landings. The next vital task was to construct bridges across the Rhine in order that more troops, equipment and supplies could be transported into the lodgement on the far side of the Rhine to prepare for a breakout. The first major Bailey bridge was completed by 2300 hours on 26th March. It was 1,174 feet in length, it floated on barges in the river and could carry loads of up to forty tons, enough to support the weight of a tank. By the time the bridge was completed, the bridgehead was thirty-five miles wide and twenty miles deep.

An example of individual bravery is given in *The Story of the RASC*. Corporal Gardner and D Platoon were working on a bridge approach and were under constant shell and mortar fire. They had to 'traverse a cutting in the flood bank, which meant that vehicles were silhouetted against the sky. This cutting was under fire by enemy Spandau guns on the opposite bank. Ignoring cover and casualties among the sappers and pioneers, Corporal Gardner stood in the cutting, directing and supervising his section. When one of the drivers faltered, he took over his truck and kept the vital supply of road-making materials flowing smoothly'. If he had not taken this brave action, the crossing of the River Rhine at this point would have been delayed. Corporal Gardner, a fellow corporal that Stan probably knew, was awarded the Military Medal for his bravery.

Within a few more days, the enemy had been pushed back a hundred miles from the Rhine and rapid advances were being made all along the battlefront.

Advancing through Germany.

After the long depressing winter of 1944/45 things were improving for the army and for Stan. The final V-2 rockets fell on London on 27th March and at last Stan did not have to worry about his family back home being blown up.

Stan loved cats so he must have been delighted to receive this morale boosting photo from Doris in March 1945, which not only included John, almost three years old, and Michael, now 8 months, but also the family cat.

By 4th April Stan had crossed one of the floating Bailey bridges at Rees and was eight miles east of the Rhine at Wetherbruch. In another five days he had travelled a further sixty miles into Germany and was near the town Rheine in a village called Welbergen. But there was danger even behind the front line as Stan heard one of his colleagues' drivers was killed near Sulingen, and at Westerwische two of his company's tippers were damaged by shellfire. Further south, Germany's industrial heartland, the Ruhr, was surrounded by Allied troops and, by 21st April, 325,000 German soldiers had surrendered from this part of the battlefield.

Stan was now rapidly advancing through Germany, but progress was difficult. As well as the occasional pocket of German resistance, the roads in many areas were in poor condition, causing accidents and breakdowns. Also, it was dangerous to stray on to the grass verges in case they had been mined. Whenever they stopped, Stan's workshop platoon would have to take over a barn or other building to set up a temporary workshop and set to work on damaged vehicles. But just as soon as they were settled in they would have to move off again to catch up with the advancing army.

By 25th April Stan was at Siedenburg between Bremen and Hanover.

Nazi atrocities. Locals taught a lesson.

Stan must have witnessed many scenes of death, injury and destruction since arriving in France. He would have seen bodies of soldiers lying by the roadside, awaiting burial, injured colleagues being taken to medical stations and death amongst the local people in bombed-out ruins of towns and villages that he drove through. These were the result of the war to liberate Europe he was involved in. What he had yet to come across was evidence of the Nazi brutality and mass extermination for purely racial or nationality reasons. This was to change.

On 15th April (John's third birthday) the leading tanks in advance of Stan reached and liberated the Belsen concentration camp. What they found was truly shocking. There were 53,000 prisoners inside, most half-starved and seriously ill, and another 13,000 corpses lying around the site, the result of deliberate brutality and neglect. The entry into Belsen was filmed by news reporters and made into a film. The film was shown across Germany where the local population was in many places forced to watch it in order to understand the savagery of the Nazi regime. By 26th May, D Platoon of Stan's company was within two and a half miles of Belsen. Those soldiers would have most likely seen the survivors clinging onto life as they were looked after by the Allied medical teams. Stan would have heard the stories from his colleagues of what they had seen of the Nazi inhumanity towards the Jews. Did Stan see the Belsen camp?

Stan's company come across the site of a massacre of prisoners in April 1945 In Soltau, Germany. Local German civilians can be seen being forced to re-bury prisoners that had been massacred by the Nazis.

On a much smaller scale, soldiers of Stan's company came across the site of a massacre near the town of Soltau on 25th April. The company war diary states 'B Platoon… saw a mass grave on the Soltau-Heber Road containing between 1,500 and 2,000 bodies, mainly Poles and Russians. The bodies were being exhumed for decent burial by civilian men and women from Soltau – many bodies had been bleeding from their noses and ears'. In reality, the numbers were much smaller than this report indicated. What appears to have happened is that prisoners from a concentration camp were being transported by train when it had to stop near Soltau as a result of an Allied air raid. Many prisoners managed to escape from the train but were then hunted down by members of the Wehrmacht, the SS and the Hitler Youth, and then they were shot. Stan, like the soldiers who made the townspeople dig up the corpses to give them a proper burial, must have been sickened on hearing about these dreadful events. Stan never spoke about the horrors he saw during the war. I wonder whether the reason why in later life he never again wanted to cross the English Channel to continental Europe was that it would revive memories of that horrific time.

While researching this massacre, I came across the Pathe News website. On this site I was amazed to find a five-minute film shot on 25th April 1945. It immediately took me back to that day when the British troops were discovering the real horror of a massacre site. It showed the local Soltau civilians digging up the bodies of the massacred prisoners and putting them in coffins for a proper burial. A British officer is seen questioning local people about the murders. The townspeople are smartly dressed in suits, ties and hats and clearly did not expect to be ordered to dig up dead bodies. The British soldiers no doubt wanted to teach the locals a lesson about the brutality of their fellow countrymen. The film is very graphic and not for the squeamish.

The war ends, Stan kept abroad, Doris moves.

Stan and his fellow soldiers knew that the war would be over soon, but there was still danger and fighting to be done. On 26th April 1945 three tipper lorries of his company were ambushed by a small party of SS soldiers. The war diary states: 'The officer was killed instantly but the drivers… were able to take cover. The enemy eventually made off with no further casualties on either side. One vehicle was slightly damaged.' It is not known how close Stan was to this incident, but he would have heard about it. He would have been aware of the danger that still existed despite the war being in its closing stages.

By 28th April the British Army had driven the Germans back to the River Elbe in northern Germany. The River Elbe was the agreed boundary between the British and American forces and their Russian allies. The only exception to the British crossing the River Elbe was near Hamburg where the British were allowed to advance to Lubeck on the Baltic. This enabled the British and Americans to have a port on the Baltic, and also satisfied Churchill's desire to deny the Russians access to Denmark. However, the Russians had not yet reached the eastern side of the River Elbe, which was still heavily defended by the Germans.

To reach Lubeck, the British had to find a way of crossing the river under fire and defeating the Germans on the other side. On the night of 28th/29th April, in what proved to be the last major British battle of the war, the British crossed the river. They used Buffaloes, a type of amphibious troop carrier, storm boats and DD tanks – tanks that could swim across rivers (DD stands for 'Duplex Drive', although they were humorously nicknamed 'Donald Duck' tanks by the troops). Despite strong resistance, the British established themselves on the other side and immediately started building a bridge across the river. Stan's company was supporting the Royal Engineers in building the bridge. The war diary states: 'The Bridge was 1,040 feet in length and was constructed in twenty-nine hours under fire'.

On the same day as the River Elbe was being bridged, the good news was announced that food was at last getting through to northern Holland. Some 3,000 British bombers were dropping food in the Rotterdam and Hague area. At last the Dutch hunger winter was coming to an end. Stan must have been delighted having seen for himself the half-starved children in southern Holland.

More good news was to follow on 30th April as Adolf Hitler, the German Chancellor, committed suicide that day. However, the danger in Germany was not over yet as on the same day, Stan's company's lorries were attacked from the air by enemy fighters near Winsen, fortunately without anyone being injured.

Stan must have thought that surely the war must soon be over. And so it was. On 4th May German forces in Holland, North West Germany and Denmark surrendered to General Montgomery near Wendisch. Surrender of other German forces took place over the next few days. The war in Europe was over. 8th May was declared 'Victory in Europe Day' and there were wild celebrations in the capitals of Europe. Stan was most likely in Rotenburg, between Bremen and Hamburg, when he celebrated the end of the war. According to the war diary, VE Day was celebrated a day late on 9th May. Was this because they heard the news late or did the celebrations go on for a second day? Stan said that winning the war had been 'touch and go'. And the more I study the war, the more I realise how close the Germans were to defeating Britain and occupying our country.

It was just a few days after the end of the war when Stan heard the news that he had been granted seven days' leave in the UK. How delighted he must have been. But the trip from the centre of Germany to the Channel ports was over worn out and damaged roads choked with refugees. It must have taken some time. So the time he spent at home was four or five days at the most. Only a short time to meet and get to know his new son, Michael, who was now ten months old. As soon as Doris had heard about Stan's leave she arranged for Michael's christening to take place at Mount Avenue Church. It was still difficult for Stan and Doris to plan for the future as the war against Japan in the Far East was still raging and there was a possibility that British troops would be sent to support the Americans in the invasion of Japan. How they must have wished Stan could have stayed at home now that the war in Europe was over, but he had to do his duty. By 29th May he was on his way back to Germany.

Stan would have become very familiar with the central square in Peine, northern Germany, where he was based for eight months at the end of the war. The photo shows the old city hall.

On 5th July Stan voted for the Conservative Party in the General Election. Stan said that Churchill 'got us through the war with his stirring speeches and strong leadership' and expected him to win as Churchill personally had an 83% approval rating. It was a shock then when Clement Atlee's Labour Party won in a landslide victory by taking 393 seats in the 640-seat Parliament. The country had been won over by Labour's promise to introduce a 'welfare state' with a free National Health Service, extended free education and a national health insurance system. Stan's forebodings about a socialist government were realised in the late 1940s as his confectionery business was held back from expansion by a myriad of government rules and controls.

In July Stan was promoted to Sergeant, albeit without extra pay. The company headquarters and workshop moved further south to Peine, some twenty-five miles south east of Hanover. Peine was a small market town with some pretty, old buildings, including the old city hall and a windmill. Stan was to be based there for the next eight months. Other platoons of the company were based at Marklohe, Nordheim and Celle to the north and south. Stan's job probably involved travelling all around this central area of Germany recovering broken down vehicles as well as repairing them in Peine. The rest of the company were busy transporting supplies and equipment and repairing roads.

Early August brought the news of the dropping of atomic bombs on Hiroshima and Nagasaki in Japan, which brought the war in Asia to an end. Stan said that dropping the atomic bomb was the right thing to do as it saved many Allied lives and brought the war to an end much quicker. It also finally removed the possibility of Stan being sent to the Far East.

The months after the end of the war must have been frustrating for Stan. Like every other soldier, he just wanted to get home. Why did he have to stay in Germany for another nine months after the end of the war? There are several answers to that question. First of all, the Allies had to make sure that the German forces did not re-establish themselves. In particular, the fanatical Nazis had to be identified and, where there was evidence of war crimes, put on trial. Secondly, the country was in chaos – whole cities had been destroyed by bombing, roads and bridges smashed. Water and power had to be restarted, roads repaired and the trains encouraged to move again. There were hundreds of thousands of displaced persons. Slave labourers and concentration camp survivors were trying to get home. Germans from the east were fleeing from the invading Russians. Ethnic Germans from other countries, where they were now being persecuted, were also seeking sanctuary in Allied-occupied Germany. Germany was in a great flux, so someone had to administer and police the country and, in the north of Germany, this fell to the British Army.

Whilst Stan no doubt appreciated that the army had to ensure that Germany developed into a peaceful and well-governed country, he must have longed to get home. There was much to do in Britain. London and many other towns had been badly damaged in the bombing, food and many other essentials were still on ration and thousands of soldiers were returning looking for work. The country was almost bankrupt as it had spent so much on the war effort and had borrowed heavily from the Americans.

Whilst Stan was in Peine in northern Germany, driving and maintaining army lorries, Doris was busy in England arranging where the family was going to live once Stan returned. The house in Mount Avenue was, most likely, rented, probably very cheaply as there were hundreds if not thousands of empty houses in the town during the war. Now the war was over, the landlord probably wanted the house back. Doris had to choose the next house without Stan's help. She decided to buy a three bedroomed semi-detached house in Westborough Road, Westcliff. My brother, Mick, and I believe the house was purchased, although it could have been rented. Doris and Stan had a joint bank account and Doris was a signatory to the business bank accounts, so she would have had access to finance. 305 Westborough Road was one of the nicer houses in an area of mainly early-twentieth century terraced properties. It had small front and rear gardens and Doris thought that Stan would be impressed that it had its own driveway to a detached garage. It had the luxury of an indoor toilet and bathroom, although the kitchen, or scullery as it was called, was tiny with only space for a sink and an oven. Stan must have been delighted when he saw the house, when on leave, for the first time in October 1945. Their own house at last, and how he must have looked forward to returning to live there once he was released from the army for good.

Stan would rather have been given home leave. However, instead he was sent to a rest and relaxation centre. This is a postcard he sent on 2nd September 1945 from Bad Harzburg, a spa town in the Harz Mountains some thirty-three miles from Peine, where his platoon was based. On his postcard Stan says:

'This is where everybody eats. There are also bars inside and out, upstairs and down. It's a palatial place, a very good band plays meal times and evenings. Entertainment is not so good here. One dance on last night, one film and no ENSA. Location and accommodation perfect. Needs Mr Butlin around! All my love from,
xxxx Stan xx'

(ENSA was the entertainments wing of the British Army. 'Mr Butlin' is a reference to the founder of Butlins Holiday Camps.)

1945. WAR ENDS, SEPARATION DOESN'T.

No wonder Stan is cuddling Michael, now fifteen months old, as this is only the second time he has seen him. John, now three and a half, appears to be developing his taste for cars. The twelve days' privilege leave in October 1945 was his longest home leave of the whole war. The setting is the driveway of their new home at 305 Westborough Road, Westcliff-on-Sea.

8. 1946. Back to normal life: death, illness, work and family.

Doris's solitary sadness, Stan's military mementoes.

Whilst Doris was anxiously waiting for the good news of when Stan was coming home, she heard of sad news. On 9th January 1946 her father, William Cockshull, died at Banstead Hospital in Surrey at the age of sixty-five. He had been in this mental institution for some years. It is not currently known why he was in there, although Queenie, his elder daughter, once said to me that William's brothers had led him astray and got him in the habit of drinking too much. (Why did I not ask more questions at the time?) Was Doris able to go to the funeral at Morden Cemetery on 17th January or was she unable to leave her two young children? Doris never spoke about her father. Was this partly because she did not know him very well, as he could have been in the mental hospital many years? Queenie only mentioned him to me a couple of times, once to explain what a skilful carpenter he was and that the lovely darkly polished chest of drawers in her living room was made by him. This bow-fronted chest of drawers was very large, standing over four and a half feet tall and four feet wide. When she was quite elderly, she moved it with her into the lounge of her ground floor flat at 20 Brightwell Avenue, Westcliff-on-Sea, even though it was much too large for the room. It was a proud reminder of her distant father.

Meanwhile, in Germany, 1st January 1946 saw 'many other ranks dispatched for release' and the 'disposal of vehicles' according to the 486 RASC Company war diary. But Stan was not amongst those released, indeed on 15th January he was transferred to RASC 575 Company Mechanical Transport, which was located in Warminster, Dorset. A week later, he was promoted to W/Sergeant (a search on Google says W stands for War, as it was only applicable during war time or just after as the army did not want too many Sergeants if they all stayed on in peace time. Another post says it meant 'Wheeler Sergeant', which is some sort of category in the army service corps). Stan told me that the army wanted him to stay on and offered him a promotion if he agreed. But Stan was having none of it and turned down the offer.

Stan's 'Service and Casualty Form' in his army records indicated that he had spent only three days in Warminster as, on 18th January 1946, he was transferred to an army unit in Stanford-le-Hope, Essex, and on the same day admitted to the Military Hospital Shoeburyness. So, the day after her father's funeral, Doris heard about the sickness of her husband. He had survived eighteen months in dangerous and unhealthy conditions in France, Belgium, Holland and Germany only to return to England and be admitted to hospital. He was discharged from hospital after ten days. The only illness I can remember Dad talking about is jaundice and I expect that is what he was in hospital for. Someone with jaundice is likely to have a yellow look to their skin and the whites of their eyes. It is often due to conditions affecting the liver, such as cirrhosis, hepatitis or gallstones. It is unclear how he caught jaundice as he was only an occasional drinker of alcohol and the army diet would have been relatively healthy.

The special day that Stan and Doris had been awaiting for so long, came on 14th March 1946 when he was released from the army and transferred to the Territorial Army Reserve. What excitement there must have been when Stan arrived, wearing civilian clothes for the first time in four and a half years, at 305 Westborough Road to be greeted by Doris, John and Michael.

He left the army with a few mementoes:

Firstly, an advance of £10 to see him on his way back into civilian life.

Secondly, a testimonial from his commanding officer which reads: 'Military Conduct – Exemplary. Testimonial – An excellent NCO, thorough and honest, sober and trustworthy. He has been employed as (i) Driver in charge vehicles (ii) Fitter motor vehicles (iii) Vehicle mechanic, and has always carried out any tasks allotted to him in an exemplary manner. He is an efficient, willing and conscientious N.C.O.'

Thirdly, Campaign medals (i) 1939–45 War Medal [note, I have two of these medals. Was one for James King?] (ii) 1939–45 Star (iii) France and Germany Star (iv) Defence Medal. Why did his children never see these medals during his lifetime? I suspect he was not particularly proud of his medals and would rather share present day experiences than think about the past.

Fourthly, a heavy, long, brown, leather, sleeveless coat that he wore in the garden on cold winter days for the next twenty-five years.

Fifthly, a model of a RAF Spitfire that he had made for his children from a one penny coin.

And lastly, memories of awful sights I suspect he had seen whilst with the army across Europe, thoughts that he wanted to forget.

Stan and Doris's early married life had been dominated by the war. They had married in June 1940 and, by the time Stan was demobbed five years and nine months later, they had only been together some eighteen months. Similarly, by March 1946 John was three years and nine months old yet Stan had been with him for less than four months. He had also missed the early months of Michael growing up. He needed to restart his married life and get to know his sons, particularly the eldest one, John, to whom he may have seemed somewhat of a stranger.

Did Stan bring back any mental scars from the war? Many soldiers were badly troubled in later life by memories of horrific war experiences. Stan never showed any signs of such troubles. To his children he was a well-balanced, positive, forward-looking person. It helped that he had not been a front-line soldier, but he must have seen many gruesome sights, having been in artillery shooting range of German guns and having suffered through Luftwaffe raids from the sky. He was stationed not far from the Belsen concentration camp and was aware of the inhumanity that went on there. However, on the few occasions he spoke about the war, there was no particular anger or hatred against the Germans, or self-pity that he had to spend five years of his life fighting them. He had moved on. It is understandable, though, that he never wanted to cross the English Channel again for a holiday. Seeing the continent again held no attractions for him. The nearest he came to criticism of the Germans was him saying that he did not want East and West Germany to reunify as they could then be a risk to the rest of Europe. He was supportive and very interested when Michael and I toured Germany for consecutive summers in the early 1960s.

Stan gets back to business.

Stan's father, Sam, and Doris had done a good job in keeping the business going during the war. The last year before Stan returned from the forces (up to Feb 1946) there was still a profit of £279. While Stan must have been pleased that the business was in such a good state when he returned to sweet making in March 1946, he must have had a real regret that he was not able to start running the business with his brother, Jim, who had been killed earlier in the war. However, Stan kept his brother's memory alive in the name of the business as it was always known as 'J and S King Limited'. Nevertheless, Stan set to work with enthusiasm. The first thing was to expand production and for this he needed larger premises, so within months of returning home, and with the help of a loan from his mother, he bought a larger factory. The following year, and the first year of Stan's running the business, saw profits rise to £337. The business accountant says in his letter of 7th March 1947 that the good results were despite 'restriction in sugar supply… and removal of the business to Ely Works' Ely Road, Southend.

Within months of returning from army service, Stan bought this factory in Ely Road, Southend-on-Sea. The wire cage later became a store for sacks of sugar. The barrels may have contained liquefied sugar called glucose. A large modern sweet factory was built in 1953 on the site in the foreground.

9. 1947 onwards. The family is complete but are dreams fulfilled?

At last, a family event enjoyed together.

Nearly five years in the army had deprived Stan of seeing his two sons develop from babies into young people, and Doris had missed the joy of sharing the bringing up of young sons. Perhaps this was the reason that a happy event occurred on Christmas Day 1947. John said he could not understand why his mum was not with them and why his aunt and grandmother were cooking the Christmas lunch. All became clear when Stan told the boys that they had a new brother. Mick remembers that he and John were both given a Dinky Toy car to celebrate the arrival of their new brother. When Stan first saw me in Rochford Hospital (as he recounted years later), he thought I looked 'even', so I became 'even Stephen' with James, after my war deceased uncle, as my middle name.

1947 ONWARDS. THE FAMILY IS COMPLETE BUT ARE DREAMS FULFILLED?

Are Doris (pregnant with me) and sons, John and Michael, amongst the families on Chalkwell Beach in 1947? The rows of concrete tank traps and other invasion defences have been removed and the sands can be enjoyed again. Note the missing iron railings and posts that were taken away to provide wartime material for tanks, aeroplanes, etc. The white building is a children's beach theatre where I used to watch Punch and Judy shows. This is the closest beach to the Mount Avenue and Westborough Road homes and I remember being taken here quite often. Can you spot the man with the knotted handkerchief on his head and the smoke from the steam train leaving Chalkwell Station?

Who's missing from my christening celebration photograph? My uncle, Jim. He would have been my godfather if he had survived the war. The picture was taken following my christening in early 1948 at St Andrews Church, Westborough Road, Westcliff-on-Sea. I am being held by my grandmother, Grace King. Also in the photo are: Doris, her mother (Harriet), Sam King, and (in the front) John, Stan and Michael. Queenie, my godmother and Doris's sister, is taking the picture.

Were Stan and Doris's wartime dreams realised?

The dreams many young people held for their future lives were shattered by the war. For example, some had lost loved ones, some had been injured themselves, or been made homeless. The country had been bankrupted by the cost of the war, food and clothing continued to be rationed, and thousands of soldiers were returning home looking for work. How could Stan's young sweet-making concern prosper when his business partner and brother had been killed in the war? How could Stan and Doris fulfil their dreams at such a bleak time?

Doris had been keeping the sweet business ticking over with her father-in-law, Sam, during the war. With all that experience, she was able to give Stan tremendous support while he was building up the business now he was back home. Doris, with her intelligence and thoroughness, was an essential element in running the firm and I believe many of the business decisions were made jointly between them. With such a hardworking and astute partnership, the business thrived, in spite of the rationing of sugar and all the bureaucratic controls and high taxes that had been imposed on businesses by the new Labour government. Sam still worked in the factory, even though he was now sixty-five years old, so he was able to keep a family eye on the factory when Stan or Doris were not there.

All prepared for winter with warm coats and hats. Boys' knees get cold, though, with short trousers. This is probably late 1949, with Michael aged five, John seven and Stephen two. Big American cars were not uncommon in Britain after the war. This is a Ford station wagon, known as a 'Woodie', with the rear body constructed on a wooden framework.

Doris was no doubt delighted when, soon after the war ended, her mother closed her ironmonger's shop in Lordship Lane, Dulwich, and retired in order to live closer to Doris. Harriet Cockshull and Doris's sister, Queenie, bought a fine Edwardian house in Finchley Road, Westcliff. Queenie continued to work in London by commuting from Westcliff station.

The pre-war fortune teller was right; Doris did have three sons. My brothers – John aged eight, Michael aged six – and me at about two and a half in 1950.

As her three sons grew up, Doris did everything she could to support them and ensure they had a good start in life. Whether it involved being up early and cooking the porridge and bacon and fried bread for breakfast or helping with our homework in the evening while working at the sweet factory during the day – she always found time. In her limited spare moments, her passion was growing things and she created a wonderful garden in the house they moved to in 1955 at Barling (some three miles from Southend). They both had to work long and hard. Stan's work involved organising and managing a factory with some thirty staff, ordering supplies, arranging deliveries, marketing, arranging banking finance as well as mixing the confectionery ingredients in large, hot, copper pans. But they saw the benefits of their hard work.

By the mid-1950s, they had the trappings of successful businesspeople: a property in the country with a couple of acres of land, a Jaguar car, and children at private schools. This period proved to be the peak of their business careers, and with a very happy family life it must have seemed that all their youthful dreams had been realised.

Evidence of better times: nice clothes, a smart car (Austin Sheerline), and Michael and I in our private school uniforms. Michael's school, Highfield College, did not allow long trousers until you were either thirteen years old or 5 feet 3 inches in height, hence the bare knees. The photograph was taken outside one of the Butlins holiday hotels in Cliftonville in Kent. The badges on our jackets were given to us each year when we visited Butlins. I was proud of how many years we had been going to the holiday camps and hotels. Wartime dangers, anxieties and deprivations had been long forgotten by the mid-1950s. Stan and Doris had achieved family contentment and business success.

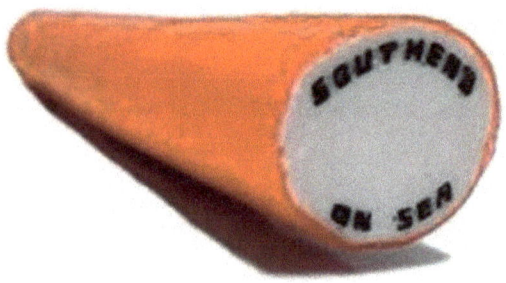

In the 1950s Stan and Doris's business was a major producer of rock, supplying almost all the seaside resorts from Skegness to the Isle of Wight. The exception was their hometown of Southend where the seafront outlets were owned by other rock makers.

This is an advertisement from a confectionery trade magazine in 1957. D Green is the agent Stan used to promote sales of his sweets. Seaside rock sold mainly in the summer so, at other times of the year, the business relied on sales through town sweetshops and newsagents. In the 1940s and early 1950s these sales were mainly of wrapped or unwrapped sweets, such as humbugs, fruit drops, candy twist, etc. sold by the ounce from glass jars. In the 1950s, Stan started making wrapped boiled sweet bars, like the ones above, which proved to be very popular. By the early 1960s, he was making 'Fizz Bars' in numerous flavours, which were a little softer and, as the name suggests, had a fizzy taste. For many years, I kept the last box of sweets he ever made (1963). However, by the early 1980s they had dissolved.

Happy years. Sudden sadness. Fatherly advice.

Stan's fatherly advice to me for happiness was 'do the ordinary things in life'. By which, I think he meant such things as 'Work hard, cultivate a happy marriage and look after the family.'

Stan and Doris certainly tried to live out that advice.

Stan worked five and a half days a week fifty-one weeks a year to make his sweet business successful. At their bungalow in Barling, he built sheds and green houses in the garden and installed central heating in the house. Doris was busy cooking, ironing, helping with homework, working in the factory and sharing with Stan the worries of running a business when times proved difficult.

Doris looked after the health of her three sons. There were many visits to the doctor's surgery and Great Ormond Street Hospital to try and resolve our problem with 'flat feet'. When I was five I had a severe swelling on my right knee which necessitated staying for many months in Black Notley Hospital. I was very proud that Mum and Dad were the only parents in my ward who visited on a Wednesday afternoon, although they had to greet all the other children individually before they came to see me.

Stan and Doris were a devoted couple. I only remember hearing them rowing once, and that was over a silly issue of using the wrong glass tumbler.

As soon as they could afford to do so, they sent their sons to private schools, although this involved sacrifices. Stan had nice cars, but they were second-hand. They hardly ever went out for meals together, and they avoided employing tradesmen. Stan did his own car repairs, house maintenance and even major jobs like putting in central heating. But, by the early 1960s, the business was declining and money was tight, although they still managed to pay the private school fees.

They did not neglect their marriage, as they made sure they had quality time together by employing a babysitter once a week so they could go to the pictures or to the Palace Theatre. Once we boys were old enough to look after ourselves in the evening, they took up their pre-war passion for ballroom dancing again.

After the death of my grandmother, Grace, in 1960, my grandfather (Sam King) moved into a caravan at our house in Barling. It must have been satisfying to Stan to be able to look after his elderly father for the last ten years of his life. However, this was somewhat difficult for Doris as there were now five men in her household. At the dinner table, when the conversation was yet again about cars or politics, she would make the plea 'can we talk about flowers and gardening for a change?'.

Sweet making had been in the family since 1878 and no doubt Stan would have loved to pass on a successful business to the next generation. It was not to be. The popularity of boiled sweets and seaside rock was declining, as chocolate and soft sweet bars became ever more available.

John probably expected to take over the family business when he started to work for his father when he left school at age sixteen. While his career path was interrupted by the closure of the sweet factory, he went on to run a successful motorcycle business.

An important legacy that Stan and Doris left to their children was a good education, which allowed Mick and I the opportunity to become accountants.

Sam lived an active life until he died aged eighty-seven, and long enough to see his great grandson, Paul.

Four years later, Doris died suddenly of a brain haemorrhage aged only fifty-eight. She lived long enough to enjoy spending time with her grandson, Paul, during his first five years.

Stan was devastated by the loss of Doris, from which he never really recovered. He did remarry but life was not easy living with someone with rheumatoid arthritis. He enjoyed attending the weddings of Mary and me, and Mick and Dionne, but was unable to go to John and Val's wedding as he was too ill. He loved being a grandfather to Paul, Daniel, Trevor, Darren, Leane, Natasha and Heidi. He died of lung cancer at the age of seventy in 1981.

Did the war cast a final fatal shadow over Stan and Doris? Stan said they only took up smoking during the war to ease the worry and stress of that dangerous period. Smoking caused Stan's lung cancer and it could have contributed also to Doris's early demise.

I was twenty-four years old when Mum died. I can never remember her being ill, yet from one day being bright and healthy and on her way with Dad to choose furniture at an MFI store to a few days later – she was gone. It was a terrible shock. The grief hung heavily on me for months if not years. The whole family – Dad, my two brothers and Auntie Queenie – we were all so sad. But it was seeing my father so melancholy and crying that was the most distressing. I never felt that I was able to have a grown-up relationship with my mum, although I loved her very much. It would have been wonderful to share the enjoyment of Mary and my children with her.

It was nine years later, when I was thirty-three, that after a year or so's illness, Dad passed away. Whilst Dad's death was terribly upsetting, I had become reconciled to losing him. Since Mum's death, I had left home, married and had two children, and I feel that I had got to know my father well as a grown-up and appreciated his good qualities. I always loved seeing and talking to him, and I think he felt the same.

Remembering Stan and Doris.

Mick and I, with Mary and Dionne, celebrated the centenary of Stan's birth in 2011 and of Doris's in 2013. As we toasted their memory with a glass of wine in a restaurant near Colchester, we imagined the joy and pride Stan and Doris would have had if they could have attended the annual family meal at Orsett Hall to meet their grandchildren (Paul, Daniel, Trevor, Darren, Leane, Natasha and Heidi) and great grandchildren (Nathan, Charlotte, Ryan, Alfie, Freddie, Grace, Chloe, Evelyn, Morgan, Lucas, Zach, Freya and Anwyn and Lowen).

10. 2013. Following Father's footsteps.

During the writing of *Humbugs and Doodlebugs* I realised that, while I was familiar with the places in and around Southend that Doris must have known during the war, I knew very little about where Stan had been sent by the army. Then, when I discovered the war records of 485 Company in the National Archives at Kew, I thought how good it would be to follow Stan's journey across Europe. This would give me a sense, albeit in a much more comfortable and safe way, of what he saw during the war. Of course, I could only imagine the devastation and carnage that he witnessed. Nevertheless, it would also be a way of celebrating and appreciating what he and thousands of other soldiers did to ensure that I and my generation have lived a life on a free and peaceful continent. My brother, Mick, was keen on sharing the journey, so we planned our trip in the spring of 2013. The daily war reports of 485 Company that I had photographed on my iPhone at Kew showed every town and village that each of the four platoons and the headquarters/workshop had stayed in from Normandy to the heart of Germany. I plotted the route on Google Maps so that we could follow Stan's journey as closely as we could. It would have been wonderful to have driven a wartime Bedford truck with camouflage markings; however, we had to settle on my BMW 325i Coupe.

No U-boat risk for us.

So, on the evening of 18th May 2013, Mick and I boarded the SS Normandie in Portsmouth for an overnight crossing to France. On the night of 13th June 1944, Stan may have also sailed from the same harbour and probably also at night to reduce the risk of strafing by German fighters or attacks by U-boat submarines. We slept in a comfortable cabin; he probably did not get any sleep at all. As we approached France, we could see pleasant sandy beaches and attractive seaside houses. He would have seen metal obstacles sticking out of the water intended to puncture the hulls of unwary boats, burnt out tanks and vehicles on the beach, smashed up houses and the remains of German gun emplacements and bunkers. We drove off the car ferry's ramp on to Oosterheim's harbour and showed our passports to enter the country. He probably drove a Bedford truck off a large landing craft into shallow water and up the beach. Any French civilians that were about would have waved him a welcome.

In awe of the first parachutists.

In the early morning of 19th May, we drove along roads no longer potholed by shelling or lined by German mines, to Pegasus Bridge. We parked our car and walked into a small eatery called the Café Gondree. The café overlooked the Caen Canal and the River Orne bridges, and was the first house to be liberated on the continent of Europe. The café has been kept just as it was in 1944, with the addition of photographs and memorabilia donated by returning veteran soldiers. We were the only customers that morning, and as we enjoyed our coffee and croissant, we imagined the scene in the early hours of 6th June 1944.

The aim was to capture the bridges over the two waterways before the Germans could destroy them. This would enable the Allied troops to advance eastwards from the Normandy bridgehead. A daring plan was devised to land six gliders carrying troops so close to the bridges that it would catch the German defenders by surprise. The first three gliders landed within yards of the bridge. This was remarkable as the landing site was little more than a hundred yards wide and the action took place in late-night/early-morning conditions.

After a short firefight, the troops captured the bridge and liberated the Café Gondree. Two further gliders landed near the Orne Bridge and that was soon captured. The sixth glider was blown off course and landed some five miles away. The first action to liberate mainland Europe had been successfully completed. Mick and I walked across the bridge spanning the Caen Canal, now renamed Pegasus Bridge in honour of the Parachute Brigade who undertook the operation. We were amazed at how five ungainly troop-carrying gliders could land in such a small space between two waterways. We were in awe of the skill of the pilots and the bravery of the soldiers.

At the end of our first day in France, we stayed in the very comfortable Mercure Hotel on the Omaha Beach golf course. I expect Stan slept under his vehicle.

Love Beach, no 'amour' in '44.

At one of the anniversaries of D-Day, probably in the 1960s, Dad and I were listening to a news report of the commemorations taking place in Normandy when he told me that he landed on Love Beach some ten days after the initial assault. As it was so unusual for Dad to talk about the war, I made a note of this conversation in an old school exercise book. And I am pleased I did, although I wished I had asked him more. Many years later, I came across the old exercise book and decided to investigate Love Beach as I had never heard of it. With a little investigation on the internet, I discovered it was the eastern section of Juno Beach, where most of the Canadian troops landed. So, it was moving for Mick and I to find Love Beach on the second day of our trip and to look at the deserted stretch of yellow sand and the calm sea and imagine how different it was some sixty-nine years earlier.

All sign of the war had long since disappeared from Love Beach. However, there was a nearby place where evidence of the war still existed. So we drove along the coast to Pont du Hoc. This is the highest point on the cliffs between the Omaha and Utah beaches, and it was the site of an heroic ascent of the cliffs, on D-Day, by American forces while under enemy fire. The German troops were protected by thick concrete in their bunkers, from where they could rain down shells on the incoming Allied ships and machine gun the Americans climbing up the cliffs. However, the area was heavily bombed by Allied warships and bomber planes. As Mick and I walked around the site, we could see many deep holes in the ground and damaged concrete gun emplacements as evidence of the ferocious battle that took place in June 1944.

Mulberry harbour, Arromanches and Southend-on-Sea.

The town of Arromanches is situated in the centre of Gold Beach, one of the two British landing beaches. It is now the main centre of D-Day interest along the Normandy Coast, due in part to the museum dedicated to the memory of the D-Day landings. We spent some time viewing the extensive exhibits, most prominent of which was a model of the Mulberry floating harbour. I particularly wanted to learn about the floating harbour as I remember Dad mentioning what a wonderful piece of engineering it was and how quickly it had been assembled after the Allied landings.

The harbour itself was made up of football pitch-sized hollow concrete rectangular cuboids that were joined together and floated about a mile out to sea off Arromanches. It was protected from the waves by a line of ships that had been deliberately sunk further out to sea. The harbour was then attached to several floating roadways leading to the shore. Up to 18,000 tonnes of supplies could be unloaded in a day. These harbours made it possible to supply and sustain the hundreds of thousands of troops assembling in Normandy after D-Day. Admiral Mountbatten (uncle of the Duke of Edinburgh) was in charge of planning for the Mulberry harbours and was pessimistic as to whether they could work at all due to the difficulty of anchoring the concrete harbours and roadways to the seabed. I was very impressed when I read on the wall of the Arromanches museum Winston Churchill's somewhat tetchy response to Mountbatten's concern: 'Let me have the best solution worked out. *Don't argue the matter.* The difficulties will argue for themselves.' And eventually Mountbatten's team of engineers did find a solution to the anchoring problem.

At the time of the D-Day landings one of the hollow concrete sections of the Mulberry harbour was being towed along the River Thames on its way to France. However, it got into difficulties and sank. This massive piece of the harbour is still lying a mile or so off the beach at Southend and is fully exposed at low tide. Dad must have noticed this relic dozens of times as he drove along the seafront. I wonder if this reminded him of Arromanches in 1944.

Mick and I booked a room above a small café on the main square of Arromanches. Below the bedroom window we could see a wartime field gun, and out to sea, the remains of the Mulberry harbour. The buildings around the square looked as if they had been rebuilt in the pre-war style and I imagined that Dad would have been familiar with this place.

Wine and gunfire for the soldiers, coffee and croissants for Mick and me.

I explained in an earlier section of the story how Dad's army company was involved in the dangerous task of transporting troops to the centre of Caen in the midst of the battle for the city. Mick and I wanted to find where in Caen the action took place, so we drove into the city centre and parked near to where the map showed us was a street called St Peter's Place.

We walked into a wide street and saw the words 'Place St Peter' on the top of a bus shelter. We had found it. There were a number of old trees lining the road, and we wondered whether these were the same trees that, according to the official daily war diary, Dad's company's vehicles sheltered under on 11th July 1944. Was Dad driving one of those vehicles that day?

Behind the trees was a line of impressive three storey houses. Were these the same houses from which the local people came to offer bottles of wine and garland the trucks with flowers? Even though we were now standing in an attractive and peaceful street, it made me feel much closer to Dad's war experience to think he may have been here sixty-nine years previously amidst the chaos and danger of a battle. We then walked around the centre of the city and admired the historic old buildings. Dad had said that Caen was 'completely smashed up'. He would have been pleased to see how well it had recovered.

Am I standing under the same trees that Dad's company had sheltered under on 11th July 1944, for protection from German attack? This is me in Place St Martin in the centre of Caen in May 2013. The houses along the street were probably the same ones from which the locals emerged to give the soldiers flowers and wine.

We understand why Dad was scared for Doris.

We left Caen and it only took us four hours to drive across northern France to St Omer. We had not been delayed by roads blocked with destroyed tanks and trucks or blown up bridges. Dad had left Caen sometime in August 1944 to follow the leading British divisions that were chasing the Germans across France. By 5th September he was in Buicourt, between Paris and Dieppe, and six days later he was in Froidment, near the Belgium border. We took a more northerly route across France than Dad had done. We had a good reason for this as we wanted to visit one of Hitler's terror weapon sites.

Mick and Steve enjoying a coffee outside a café in the centre of Caen in May 2013. Dad had said that Caen was 'completely smashed up'. We mused how pleased he would have been at the way the city had been restored.

Dad had commented to me that he was more worried about Doris's and his two son's safety in Southend than for his own safety in France. One reason for this was the V-1 flying bombs and V-2 rockets that were raining down on southern England. Our next stop was one of the world's first missile launch facilities, which according to the guidebook would be used to 'destroy London'.

Soon after leaving St Omer and driving through the pleasant French countryside, Mick and I spotted a large concrete construction on the side of a hill. It had a dome of a similar shape to the O^2 concert centre in London but had a much more sinister use. This was La Coupole near Wizernes.

We parked the car, went to the entrance, paid our fee and were directed along a long tunnel into the side of a hill. There were other tunnels to each side – this was an underground city that would be safe from RAF bombing. The tunnels, we learned from the official brochure, had been dug by mainly Russian and Eastern European slave labour. The slaves were made to work in inhumane conditions and many died in the construction of this facility.

We took a lift 42m up to the main area under the dome and ahead of us was a V-2 rocket standing probably some fifty to sixty feet tall. It looked very modern, just like a large version of the Trident missile launched from present day nuclear submarines. We learned that the rockets were to be fuelled, the bomb explosive primed, the aiming mechanism set to target London, and all under this dome. The rockets would then be transported a few hundred yards to a launch pad ready for firing.

The whole process was like a production line of a modern car factory enabling an incessant barrage of rockets to fall on London. Fortunately, the RAF became aware of this site and bombed it many times. The 72m diameter dome of La Coupole was made of 5.5m thick concrete and was strong enough to withstand the Allied bombs. However, the roads and railway leading to the site were more vulnerable and the repeated attacks from the air made the site unusable. This and other fixed launch sites were abandoned by the Germans, who instead used mobile launchers, which were much more difficult for the Allied bomber aircraft to find and attack. Fortunately, La Coupole was overrun as the British advanced across northern France and never used. However, attacks continued from mobile launch sites in Germany and Holland, almost until the end of the war. The final V-2 and V-1 attacks were on 27th and 28th March 1945 respectively, according to the *FlyingBombsandRockets* website. Southend was hit by a total of five V-1 flying bombs and two V-2 rockets, according to my research at the Essex Records Office.

I left La Coupole with an appreciation of how determined the average British soldier, like Dad, must have been to advance into Germany to put an end to these terror weapons that were attacking loved ones back home.

Bomb holes and roadside mines for Dad, motorways for us.

After La Coupole, Mick and I crossed into Belgium, east of Dunkirk. We then skirted Bruges, travelled through Ghent, passed north of Brussels and encountered very heavy traffic through Antwerp. After a long day, we reached Hasselt in eastern Belgium to spend the night at the Holiday Inn Express. Dad's 486 Company had reached Bierghes, south of Brussels, by 18th September 1944 and Oostham, eighty miles to the north east, two days later. We were back on Dad's route as Oostham was just nineteen miles away.

On Thursday 23rd May 2013 we took a break from following Dad's wartime route and visited the Zolder motor racing circuit. It was here in the 1970s that Mick and our eldest brother, John, had ridden their Vincent motorcycles to the Lion rally and Mick wanted to see again the circuit and where they had stayed. We stopped in Zolder town and queued up in a baker's shop to buy some sandwiches. A very concerned local Dutchman had noticed a car with English number plates parked in the square and had come to find us to warn us of the very officious traffic warden that would soon spot that we had no parking permit. We left the area in a hurry but not before noticing that there seemed to be no old buildings in the town. *Had all the pre-war buildings been destroyed in the conflict?* we wondered.

Any pre-war buildings?

On 10th October 1944 Dad's workshop moved to Eindhoven. He was to be based there for the next five months. This was due to the Allies being unable to make significant progress due to the ill-fated attack on Arnhem; the German counter-attack called the 'Battle of the Bulge'; and the difficulty of trying to cross the heavily defended River Rhine. Perhaps in hindsight Mick and I should have spent some time in Eindhoven, getting to know the place Dad must have known well. However, we decided to move north to visit a town where there is more obvious evidence of the war, Arnhem.

On the way we wanted to visit the villages in the area between Eindhoven and Nijmegen where the other platoons of Dad's company had been based. During the five months Dad was in this area, he would probably have driven to each of the other platoon bases to collect and repair broken down vehicles or to deliver supplies. We visited Geldrop, Deurne, Beugen and Uedem. We wanted to find some pre-WW2 buildings that Dad may have also seen. But we saw none in these villages. *Were all these villages smashed up in the war? I wondered.* If so, it was very sad.

We moved on, hoping to find some villages untouched by the war. The crossing of the River Rhine was a significant achievement for the Allies so it was with some excitement that we drove across the Rhine bridge at Rees. Just across the other side was the village of Werth in Germany and at last we found an old building, a magnificent windmill, that Dad would have recognised.

At last, I find a pre-war building, on 25th May 2013, that Dad would have recognised. This is the windmill at Werth, east of the River Rhine. His company reached here on 1st April 1945. This was nine days after British and Canadian forces first crossed the Rhine at Rees and Wesel.

Brave soldiers, brave Arnhem people, starving children.

We arrived in Arnhem late in the afternoon and booked into the Best Western Hotel. The long day had given me an appetite and, to compensate, I overate on a dish of pork satay, chips and extra vegetables in the hotel restaurant. The following morning we walked the Arnhem 'Freedom Trail' that marks all the significant places during the battle for the city. 12,000 British and Polish soldiers parachuted into Arnhem to capture the bridges over the River Rhine that would have enabled the Allies to gain access to northern Germany and possibly end the war by the end of 1944.

It was moving to see the John Frost Bridge over the River Rhine. Once Major John Frost and his small group of soldiers had captured the bridge, they heroically tried to hold on to it against overwhelming opposition. The Battle of Arnhem Information Centre was just next to the bridge. It was almost empty when we arrived and we spent some time in there reading the eyewitness – British, German, Dutch and Polish – accounts of the battle. The curator (born in the same year as me, 1947) explained with some emotion the hunger and starvation that the townspeople and the rest of the Dutch population had suffered during what became known as the 'hunger winter' of 1944–45.

Once the main body of paratroopers had failed to relieve the troops at the Arnhem Bridge, they fell back a few miles to Oosterbeek and an area around the Hartenstein Hotel. Later in the morning, we visited this hotel, which is now the Airborne Museum. In the garden is a plaque that was erected by the veterans on the fiftieth anniversary of the battle. It brought tears to my eyes reading it. It read as follows:

TO THE PEOPLE OF GELDERLAND

50 years ago British and Polish Airborne soldiers fought here against overwhelming odds to open the way into Germany and bring the war to an early end. Instead we brought death and destruction for which you have never blamed us.

This stone marks our admiration for your great courage, remembering especially the women who tended our wounded. In the long winter that followed your families risked death by hiding Allied soldiers and airmen, while members of the Resistance helped many to safety.

You took us then into your homes as fugitives and friends
We took you forever into our hearts
This strong bond will continue
Long after we are all gone
1944-September-1994

After lunch in the upmarket museum café, we drove the few hundred yards to the Allied war cemetery. Here we walked among the 1,700 headstones to pay our respects to those who died in the battle. Each September there is a commemoration at the cemetery where the townspeople and school children gather to pay their respects. Every child is given a single flower to lay on each grave. What a wonderful thing to do to teach the next generation of the sacrifices made to ensure their freedom. It was a lesson the journey to Holland also taught me.

I had some regret, as Mick and I drove to the Hook of Holland to catch the overnight car ferry back to Harwich, that we had not seen all the places Dad had seen. We had not reached the towns where he spent most of his time in Europe. By April 1945 he was in Siedenburg, Germany, and then in Rotenburg until 23rd July. From then on, until sometime in the early months of 1946, he was based in Peine, east of Hanover. What were these places like and what did Stan do there in the ten months or so he was in post-war Germany? I hope to find that out on my next trip.

Tolerance, Gratitude, Admiration.

The journey had given me a sense of pride in the part Dad had played in the freeing of Europe that has endured ever since 1945. Maybe Stan did not fully appreciate the significance of the British war effort, which we can appreciate from this more distant time. Understandably, many of his generation blamed the Germans for an unnecessary war which, in Stan's case, cost him the loss of almost five years of family life and his only brother. Dad said that one of the most important human qualities is tolerance, and I never heard him show any animosity towards the German people. I left Holland humbled at the sacrifices made by my parents' generation.

Acknowledgements

Thanks to my wife, Mary, for all her thoughts and comments; to my brother, Mick, for his reminisces and suggestions; to my daughters (Heidi for her profound comments and Natasha for her strong encouragement); and to Sylvia Smith (who painstakingly reviewed the late drafts). Thanks also to Richard Burch at R2Digital for the work on the photographs and maps, to Chris Hobbs for his assistance on the Beighton Rail Disaster and to Leila Green at Iamselfpublishing for all her support.

Photograph Acknowledgements

All photographs are the author's, other than the following. Thanks is given for their use.
Southend-on-Sea map background, Bing.
Bombing raid 1940, Southend Pictorial.
Newspaper report, Finchley Road, Essex Record Office.
Southend Police Station, Essex Record Office.
Troop train accident photograph, Railways Archives.
Troop train accident report, Manchester Guardian.
James King accident report, Southend Standard.
Southend promenade bomb damage, Essex Record Office.
Bombed houses Fleetwood Avenue, Essex Record Office.
Normandy map background, Bing.
Bretton Woods plaque, Northern New England Villages.com.
Eindhoven bomb damage, 506th Airborne Infantry Regiment Association.
Eindhoven liberation, Jacob van Slooten.
France to Holland map background, Bing.
Soltau mass grave, British Pathe.
Chalkwell Beach 1947, Francis Frith.

Bibliography

Arnhem 1944, Martin Middlebrook, Pen and Sword 1994
Arnhem 1944, Stephen Bardsey, Osprey 1993
Arromanches: History of a Harbour, Alain Ferrand, Orep 1997
British Army Handbook 1939–45 by George Forty, Sutton Publishing 1998
Bombers and Mash, Raynes Minns, Virago Press 1980
Caen 1944, Ken Ford, Osprey Publishing 2004
Christmas on the Home Front, Mike Brown, The History Press 2004
D-Day Atlas, Charles Messenger, Thames and Hudson Ltd 2004
D-Day 1944: Gold and Juno Beaches, Ken Ford, Osprey Publishing 2002
D-Day 1944: Sword Beach and the British Airborne Landings, Ken Ford, Osprey Publishing 2002
D-Day: The Battle for Normandy, Antony Beever, Penguin Books 2010
D-Day: The Story through Maps, Richard Harper, Times Books 2014
D-Day to Berlin, Andrew Williams, Hodder and Sloughton 2004
Essex at War, Frances Clamp, Pen and Sword 2017
Essex Ready for Anything, Michael Foley, Sutton Publishing 2006
German V-Weapon Sites 1943–45, Steven J Zaloga, Osprey Publishing 2008
History of Southend, Ian Yearsley, Phillimore & Co 2001
Into the Reich-Battles on Germany's Western Frontier 1944–1945, James Arnold/Badsey/Ford/Zaloga, Osprey Publishing 2002
La Coupole, Yves Le Maner, La Coupole Editions 2011
Order of Battle Western Allied Forces of WWII, Michael E Haskew, Amber Books 2009
RAF Southend 1940–1944, Peter C Brown, The History Press 2012
Rhine Crossing 1945, Ken Ford, Osprey Publishing 2007
Southend at War, Dee Gordon, The History Press 2010
Second World War – a Complete History, Martin Gilbert 2004
Story of the Royal Army Service Corps, published under the direction of the Institute of the Royal Army Service Corps by G Bell and Sons Ltd, 1955
Victory in Europe, Julian Thompson, Imperial War Museum 1995
With the Jocks, Peter White, Sutton Publishing Ltd 2004

Sources and Notes

Introduction

Playground games for my generation, fear and tragedy for my parents' generation
–Number of soldiers –*Answers.com*

Chapter 2

Stan's grandfather spots a business opportunity
  –'sweet making history', *candyhistory.net* and *Who Do You Think You Are?* magazine, August 2017
'Cokernut' toffee at the seaside
  –'enough to buy a house', Office for National Statistics Table 502
  –'unemployment', *British Unemployment 1919–1939* by W Garside 1990

Chapter 3

Invasion Preparations, evacuation precautions, Spitfire heroics
  –'Rented a shop at 505 London Road'. *The Southend Standard* reported the death of James King eight days after the train accident. In that report it mentions two business premises, 488 and 505 London Road, Westcliff-on-Sea. The former is the factory in Shoe Lane behind 488, and 505 is the shop they rented to sell their sweets. The annual business accounts show that they only paid rent for the shop for one year of 1940.

Chapter 4

Confectioner to soldier
- '3m men in the army', *British Army Handbook 1939–45* by George Forty Sutton Publishing 1998
- 'driving licences…first day issued', Motor Car Act 1903. Sam King III said he queued up on the first day driving licences were issued in 1903: 'If I had got up earlier I would have had a lower number on my licence,' he jokingly told me.

Chapter 5

A unique tragedy – the Beighton Train Disaster
- Royal Artillery… Shoebury Barracks, *Southend at War* by Dee Gordon.

Invasion training, home alone, and pregnant
- Gas Masks. These were officially called respirators. By the end of the war a staggering 97 million General Civilian Respirators had been produced, two for every member of the population. *Britain at War* magazine, August 2018.

Chapter 6

D-Day and the start of freeing Europe
- '30 Battleships…' *Campaign D-Day 1944*(4)
- '160,000 Soldiers…' *Wikipedia*

No Stan, another family event, plenty of danger
- 'Joan Rhodes awaiting the birth of her first child' BBC WW2 *People's War* Article ID A1137368

Chapter 7

- Soltau Massacre…*British Pathe news, forum.axishistory.com,* and *Wikipedia*

Chapter 10

Following Father's footsteps
- '18,000 tonnes'. D-Day Museum Arromanches Museum Guide
- V-1 and V-2 numbers. Essex Records Office

General Sources

–The National Archives, Daily War Records 486 Company RASC
–*Wikipedia*
–Essex Records Office
–*answers.com*
–*beyondessex.co.uk*
–*dday-overlord.com* (daily chronicle of the battle for Normandy)
–*Flyingbombsandrockets.com*
–*measuringworth.com* (pre-war values and prices)
–*railwaysarchive.co.uk*
–*rootschat.com*
–*southendstandard.co.uk*
–*southendtimeline.com*
–*ww2Talk.com, RASC Forum*

About the Author

Stephen James King was born in 1947 and grew up in Southend-on-Sea. As a child he remembers wrapping sticks of rock at his parents' sweet factory, and playing in an abandoned Second World War anti-aircraft compound. Both experiences sparked an interest and curiosity that continues to this day. He is a retired accountant, finance director and company chairman, and currently undertakes community work as the lead governor on an NHS Trust. He lives (within range of the battleship Bismarck's guns were it cruising off Southend Pier) with his wife, Mary. They have two daughters, three granddaughters and two grandsons.

Please send information or comments relating to this story to

stevejk88@outlook.com

www.ingramcontent.com/pod-product-compliance
Lightning Source LLC
Chambersburg PA
CBHW042035100526
44587CB00030B/4435